"And her prophets have daubed them with untempered mortar, seeing vanity, and divining lies to them, saying, thus said the Lord GOD, when the LORD has not spoken." Ezekiel 22:28

It is my prayer to you, oh Lord, that the words I write are not from my insolent pride or trying to make other humans happy, but that they would be words inspired by you, to change this prideful and arrogant nation, to turn their ways back to the Lord, and to understand that all that we have accomplished and all the blessings we have, are inspired by you and have nothing to do with the minds and hands of men. For through you, men are brought to great heights, and at the snap of a finger, men fall from grace. Therefore, let us as a nation and world remember you, live through you, and learn that by which is right.

Introduction

I wrote this book to share thoughts on my interpretation of the Bible and of life. As time goes on, it seems that mankind finds more and more reasons to ignore the basic tenants of the Bible. To me, as a father of 4, a Police Officer, small business owner, and Reserve Army Officer, I do not understand. I mean, from the beginning of the country when General George Washington and General De Lafayette were fighting at Yorktown, Virginia, Divine Providence was evident (when Lord Cornwallis' chance for retreat and living to fight another day was thwarted by his ships for retreat being blown downstream by an odd wind.) This is just one example of the divine providence that helped to create this great and mighty country out of basically nothing. We have over the last 235(+) years been blessed with relatively few depressions, clean water, food, a steady source of employment, and for the most part, peace.

Today, 2012, I see children being raised that it is better to cheat and win, than to play fair and lose. I see teachers who would rather cheat, and appear to have increased students test scores, than to make children work hard for the same results.

Everyone seems to be taking the easy way out. People are rapidly lining up for welfare and unemployment benefits, instead of struggling to make ends meet. The word "family" is being construed to mean whatever exists. A mother, a father, and children rarely live together. Communities are full of transient people; in fact most people who live in a community do not even know the names of their next door neighbor. Senior leaders of government and business are constantly in the paper for unethical behavior, which includes a lot of lewd behavior including child molestation, adultery, stealing, and embezzlement: but never for just lying. No one ever accuses a senior executive of simply lying anymore, although they do it more and more every day, and will continue. It is like senior executives are expected to lie or cheat; and no one cares. The year 2012 is a spectacular time of change and movement in the world. Unusual weather, earthquakes, economic instability, government and business bankruptcy, terrorism, rogue pirates, large number of fish and bird death for no reason; what does it all mean? The answers are in the Bible. It is my desire to urge you to read the Bible from Genesis to Revelations again. To teach your family its tenants, and to acknowledge that all of its contents are important for healthy living. It is my prayer that something I say might change your heart to more closely walk with God. And, finally it is my prayer that we as a nation will fall on our knees and ask God for forgiveness for overlooking homosexuality, for condoning sin, and for allowing the beautiful and secure country that he gave us to be taken over by evil.

Untempered Mortar

The first substantial government in the Bible was structured under Joseph when the Pharaoh of Egypt had a strange Dream. Basically in Genesis, Chapter 41, Verse 1 it states, "and it came to pass at the end of two full years, that Pharaoh dreamed: and behold he stood by the river. And behold, there came up out of the river seven well favored kine (cows) and fat fleshed; and they fed in a meadow. And, behold seven other kine came up after them out of the river, ill-favored and lean fleshed, and stood by the other kine upon the brink of the river. And the ill favored and lean fleshed kine did eat up the seven well favored and fat kine. So Pharaoh awoke."

From there, Joseph, the son of Jacob (Israel) was able to interpret the dream as being that Egypt was to face seven prosperous years, and then to face seven years of famine. He was then placed over the land of Egypt. And Joseph took up the fifth part of the land of Egypt in the seven plenteous years, and kept this food for the famine of the land when the seven bad years came.

Now, this makes sense. Having the most intelligent, honest,

and blessed of men to be over the finances and food supplies for a country, so that in bad years the country would be alright.

In America right now, we are in the bad years. However, I don't know they will be over in seven years, or how it will end. The truth is, we have had our prosperous years; and we did not put food in the storage bins like we should have in our good years, and now we are borrowing from smarter countries to get through the famine. And much of the wealth that we did try to store away, was under the management of non-honest managers who did not store away with the full faith and confidence of consumers, or citizens of the United States Government.

However, it has not always been that way. To begin with, America started with a group of men who had a vision. They wanted freedom of religion, but understood they could not have freedom from religion because they knew they were dependent. George Washington understood fully that to have a functional government required the Bible and a belief in God. They (founders) understood serving their country for the good of men, but they did not want anything in return. They believed in God and a greater good for all. They wanted men to be pious, and to be hard working and consistent. All of these men were required to serve their country in the militia. None of these men received Social Security, Welfare, Disability, or Small Business Assistance. Yet they lived comfortably into old age, owned small businesses, and did not expect any help. All of these men were willing to take risks, and this was shown by their taking a ship from England and travelling to an undiscovered land, and then the next generations spreading West toward California, to try to get a better life for their families. Many of these men were very poor, and had families that lived off the land, finding birds, plants or anything else they could to eat. But, these men were more likely to share the little they had with each other, than to ever steal from each other. And, their lives were lived more for the support of others, than for the support of themselves.

By the end of this book, I want to convince you that for our nation to once again be strong; for our land to once again be the land of milk and honey it has been over the last 200 years, that we need to get our men back to who they were when they began this great country. We need to elect men in office like the original men we had. We need men who are like Joseph; who have understanding. We need men who have strong moral values, and that understand right from wrong, and that are willing to be obedient and fearful of God. We need men with vision and that are willing to take chances for the future of this country, and for others in this world. And, what this risk taking and vision includes is not only the need to start new businesses and hire new employees, but also that men and women who can afford to, give up Social Security, Medicare, Medicaid, and other government subsidies in order to allow the country to provide these services to those that cannot do without them. I am not asking those who need these services to give them up. But, if you are a millionaire, and have a couple of million dollars in the bank, do you really need disability income from the government? And, would a 20% tax rate for you as well as the worker at McDonalds be too much to ask? 20% is what Joseph collected to store away.

As would be normal, I expect many people to think I am nuts; that there is no reason to give up things for other people.

After all, that is against all rational thinking during this period of our lives (2012 and beyond). My only response to this would be to quote Jesus, "But many *that are* first shall be last; and the last first." Mark 10:31.

Chapter 1

I enlisted in 1986 in the Marine Corps. As a young man with no clue what to really do with my life; it gave me a direction. In fact, when I went in the Marine Corps recruiting office, I told them I did not care what job I had in the military. I just wanted a job. I had spent the previous year since getting out of high school flipping steaks at a steak house, and putting fish in a fryer at a Seafood Restaurant. I used to come back to my mother's house after work at this seafood restaurant, and my mother would actually make me take my clothes off under the carport because I smelled so much like fish. One time, I actually stuck my hand completely under 400 degree grease while cooking fish in this restaurant, and the owner of the restaurant just wanted me back at work the next day. He had no sympathy or desire for my best interest: just a desire for survival of his business. And, as an employee needing to have a job, I would have gone back to work the next day even if my hand fell off. I showed up the next day to work with a bandage over my hand; cutting fish and performing my job the best way possible for fear of being fired. I needed a job and did not want to fail; and as I look back at it the owner of the business depended on me to be at work. This is how tough it gets sometimes in the dog eat dog world of running a small business.

However, as an employee, it started me thinking that somehow, sometime, and in some way, I could do better. One day, for a reason I still don't fully know, I walked into a Marine Corps Recruiting office and spoke to a Recruiter. This began day 1 of my life. It was my rebirth. The Marine Corps was my stepping stone to a better life. I still will tell anyone today that the Marine Corps was, is, and will forever be the greatest organization in the world. The Marine Corps Recruiter put me in Supply. I remember thinking when I was put in this Military Occupation Specialty, "I wonder what Supply is." Well, it basically is the logistical network for the United States Marine Corps. And, although I did not know it, it fit my personality right.   In 1990, after serving 4 years as an enlisted soldier, I

was tired. I wanted to go back to college. I was Honorably

Discharged at the end of my contract, and I used my GI Bill to

start college at the University of North Carolina at Pembroke. I

at this time had no plans to go back in the military. However,

with money low and needing a job, I enlisted in the NC National

Guard in 1991, because joining the Marine Corps Reserve would

take driving about 100 miles each way. The National Guard has

helped me provide for my family over the last 23 years. I have

deployed twice with them, and have travelled around the

world with them. The National Guard is a great organization

just like the Marine Corps. I will never forget my first drill at

the Lumberton, NC armory. I trained with the unit as a Cavalry

Scout frequently at Fort Bragg, North Carolina and elsewhere,

and tried to find someone who would talk to me. I was an

outsider in this organization, as well as not known, and it was

not easy to make friends. And, many of the soldiers in this

armory were from Lumberton, NC. I grew up outside of

Charlotte, NC so I sort of did not fit in. Furthermore, I always

have been and always will be what is defined as an introvert.

As we stood in formation, I stood at attention as Marines do, and tried to learn the National Guard vision. The equipment in the Armory, like some of the soldiers, were old. However, this organization, that was composed of men and women age 18-60, was an organization that was ready for war; and proved that during Operation Iraqi Freedom during two deployments. I used to ride in these old trucks (2.5 tons from the 1950's) to Fort Bragg, NC and would think "wonder if we are going to break down?" In 2004 I took a convoy of these same trucks from Kuwait to Diyala Province, Iraq and wondered the same thing as I travelled North. I was a Company Commander then and had responsibility for about 50 vehicles and trailers, as well as the soldiers and equipment inside of these trucks. However, those wonderful trucks, most made in the 1950s, made it North safely, and none of them broke down. And, when we left Iraq in 2005, we left those trucks in Iraq. I believe they wound up being used in Iraq by the Iraqi Army. And, we got new trucks when we got back into the US, which were used for training for our next deployment in 2008.

I have learned to love the National Guard as much as the

Marine Corps. The National Guard as we know it today is actually what has evolved from the original Militias, which were formed when the country was founded. And, the militias were originally derived from the Republic of Greece almost 2800 years ago. [1] The concept was the men and women would work and raise their families, and focus on this family unit and its survival until needed for the country. Then, when the country

---

[1] Few Americans know that we have two armies and that both are acknowledged by the United States Constitution. One is the military that we know best, the regulars: the U.S. Army and the U.S. Navy, joined later in history by the Marines and the Air Force. The other, originally known as the militia, is now called the National Guard. Why would our Founding Fathers invite confusion and duplication by creating two separate military establishments? The answer dates to the earliest city-state republics in Greece. Throughout 2,800 years of republican theory and practice, a standing army has always been considered a threat to republican liberty and a potential instrument of tyranny. A standing army composed, necessarily, of professional soldiers rather than citizen-soldiers represented too convenient an instrument of power for a putative dictator, tyrant or "man on a white horse." Article: **A Well-Regulated Militia:** The National Guard, not the military, should protect the homeland. By Gary Hart, November 1, 2003.

needed them they reported immediately for its selfless service until such time as they could go back home and be farmers, lawyers, teachers, etc. again. The National Guard is just like that today. We have a group of men and women who work full time for such entities as the local Police Departments, Law Firms, Banks, Retail Stores, Restaurants, and other businesses, except for 1 weekend a month, or two weeks a year, when they wear the Army uniform and become full time soldiers. And, since 9-11, many of these soldiers have deployed 2, 3 and more times in support of this country.

To begin constructing a building, you must have a strong foundation. You must have strong mortar, straight and planned walls, and good materials. The foundation is the most important part of the building. Likewise, the foundation of building effective young people is teaching them to be honest, making them strong and smart, and teaching them a trade. There is no place better for this than our United States Military Industrial Complex. Unfortunately, most individuals who are leading our financial institutions, government organizations, and other businesses do not have training in the military, which stresses the importance of telling the truth, carrying those weaker than you are, not leaving a brother or sister behind during a battle or on the home front; something so simple, so profound, yet so forgotten.

I believe that all individuals who graduate (or don't) from high school should be forced to serve (2) years in the military. If you are a kid smart enough to go straight to college (i.e. a Teacher, accountant, lawyer, dentist, etc.), then stay in school and serve 2 years when you get your degree within your occupation. The military needs these college earned skills. If you don't finish high school, you still go in the military, and the military should help you get your GED. Causing all young people to go into the military, is the beginning of making our mortar (building blocks) stronger as it makes people learn how to tell the truth, and take care of their fellow soldiers. And, the friends that they meet are so beneficial to molding your future. I just completed a course in Joint Professional Military Education at the National Defense University this year, that had the most intelligent and strongest minds I have ever seen in my life. I was amazed at their intelligence. Being around them made me think that I will never again underestimate

this country, our resolve to fix problems make solutions that

are feasible for all. We have the mental power to make things

happen. I have seen that mental power in action.

Therefore, it is my opinion that the beginning of problems

(untempered mortar) that we have in America begins with us

not making all individuals serve the military for at least 2 years,

to pay the country back for the future benefits they will be

receiving to live in this great country.

Other mortar that I believe effects our lives are as follows:

1.   Christ is the Plumbline and Cornerstone that keeps

America in check. Through him are laws to better life,

and forgiveness of ourselves and others. Without him is

a trust in the human capacity to do good, which does

not work. For example, over the last thirty years, we

have allowed prayer to be put out of school, the

teaching of the Ten Commandments in school to be

thought of as wrong, and for moral values and telling

the truth to be below success. I mean, in today's world

if you can succeed by lying, you are better than the

person who fails trying telling the truth. The problem is,

this is not true through God's eyes, and this is the

standard. The truth is that a fear of God is the

beginning of understanding. When you can

conceptualize that everything that you are, everything

that you have and want, can be given to you by

almighty God, the creator of this universe and beyond,

and he can as freely take it away. This lack of morality

is seen perhaps nowhere more clearly than by the

teachers in the Atlanta, Georgia school system that

actually lied for their students to raise test scores. How

is this better than a true report that we can work to

improve? I believe men and women from their

inception are born with the capacity to sin and to do

evil, and that they will sin unless

they pray, ask for forgiveness, and are taught moral

values.   And, children need to be taught from an early

age to fear God, and to understand what God's Laws

are. [2]

2.   If you are homosexual, don't tell anyone. You should

be ashamed. I am not saying that because I am in a

position to judge. I assure you I am a sinner and I am

not in a position to judge. But, I am in a position to

read and believe in the Bible, and fear our Holy maker,

and the Bible says it is wrong, just like sins I do are

wrong. If you are homosexual in the military, I won't

ask, and you don't tell. Once again, this will be argued,

but Sodom and Gomorrah was destroyed for

Homosexuality. I believe it is a mental disease. Just

---

[2] Come, children, listen to me. I will teach you the fear of the LORD. Psalms 34:11

like many people have Post Traumatic Stress Disorder

after serving in war zones, or are paranoid

schizophrenic, or are bi-polar, many people are

homosexual. It is not natural, just like to have other

mental disorders is not natural. [3]

3. If you can't find a job in your field, take a job in another

field, even if it is in fast food. Take a job. Currently,

there are a lot of people looking for a job. It is a

difficult time to be out of work. My daughter is in

college and has had to struggle to find a part time job.

A great movie I saw recently regarding this is called

"The Company Men." This movie discusses the problems

proud and lethargic senior executives have when they

---

[3] A Pentagon document classifies homosexuality as a mental disorder, decades after mental health experts abandoned that position. The document outlines retirement or other discharge policies for service members with physical disabilities, and in a section on defects lists homosexuality alongside mental retardation and personality disorders. Critics said the reference underscores the Pentagon's failing policies on gays, and adds to a culture that has created uncertainty and insecurity around the treatment of homosexual service members, leading to anti-gay harassment. Pentagon spokesman Lt. Col. Jeremy M. Martin said the policy document is under review. Article, USA Today, By Lolita C. Baldur, Associated Press Writer, June 20, 2006.

are laid off or fired from a job or project. One individual, who was a senior executive, went from directing a sales force to where the best job he could find was hanging sheet rock with his brother in law. One of the key facets of the movie, that you have to pay attention to for understanding, is this individuals shedding of his pride. While he was a sales executive, he had membership to a local country club. When he was laid off, his wife could not afford the country club membership and he was forced to give it up. He was like a child, in that he would have rather kept this membership than to pay his bills. How many of us act like children when we have to give things up?

Pride is the downward spiral of man.[4]

Teach Jesus in Public Schools Again

I brought this up with a couple of friends of mine at lunch this weekend, and they treated me like I was insane. Their arguments began with the basics: (1) freedom of religion,

---

[4] Proverbs 16:18 tells us that "pride goes before destruction, and a haughty spirit before a fall." Proverbs 16:18 and also "a man's pride will bring him low." Psalms 29:23

(2) forced religion on atheists, (3) people are going to sin

anyway, (4) how do I know it will help anything anyway?

(5) What about forcing Jesus on Muslims or Jewish people?

(6) All preachers want is your money.

These are all great arguments from a partly Constitutional

Point of view, as well as other humanistic points of view.

And I believe in the Constitution. However, our children

are growing up to learn it is better to cheat, lie, or steal and

pass then to work hard or fail. Our adults, as was recently

seen in Atlanta, Georgia, feel it is better to help children cheat

and pass, than to let them fail. [5] And, what does all this

cheating raise children up to become? Administrators that

believe it is alright to purchase items on Government Credit

Cards, and then return them for personal cash. Or, Financial

Advisors who lie, and steal money from others. Or, Police

---

[5] Award-winning gains by Atlanta students were based on widespread cheating by 178 named teachers and principals, said Georgia Gov. Nathan Deal on Tuesday. His office released a report from the Georgia Bureau of Investigation that names 178 teachers and principals – 82 of whom confessed – in what's likely the biggest cheating scandal in US history. Christian Science Monitor, Patrick Johnson, Tuesday, July 5, 2011.

Officers who blackmail people or let their friends off with drunk driving, while charging others. Or, a President who thinks oral sex is not adultery, although Jesus went as far as to say that to look at another woman with lust is adultery. As God sits above and looks down upon us, his creation, he sees a world of sin. And, he always has since their inception. He is aware of man's weakness, and I am not going to sit under a gourd and wait for the destruction of mankind like Jonah. We all have weaknesses. But, I know he wants more. He is not completely disgusted I believe; but upset just the same. You see he wants us to do better. We spend as a country millions of dollars a year to research food and nutrition products for our children in schools so we ensure they get proper nutrients at school. We research science, agriculture, the human body, space, and a myriad of other topics to try to increase our knowledge and understanding. Yet, we never research moral values and trying to teach young people the importance of truth, productivity and working, versus laying around playing video games, waiting for the government to pay for their lack of productivity. This is a tragedy that seemingly has no answer, unless we go back to

the basics; hard work for an honest paycheck.   Furthermore,
to combat our children's earlier and earlier fascination with sex,
instead of preaching on the sin of adultery in school we hand
out condoms like band aids. Make sure you wear your condom.
How about a little truth like adultery is a sin, and it separates
your soul from your natural ability to communicate with God.

The Draft

Like I said before, I believe we need a draft. I personally
believe it is the spark that the country needs to rebound.   We
need to take all citizens as they turn 18 or graduate from high
school and put them through military training. And, my focus
would be on putting those who drop out of high school or have
been in trouble into the US Marine Corps, with the creation of a
special GED program. There is no one that could more
effectively train and equip a young man or woman with high
school skills, as well as life and military skills, than a Marine
Corps Drill Instructor. I believe we would need enough people
teaching this program to where individual attention could be
given to those with dyslexia and other learning disabilities. And,
if someone has a physical deformity to where they could not

serve in the military, I would re-build the civil defense, and have these people participate in the manufacturing of munitions and other DOD projects. There is a lot of work that these people could do for the defense and strengthening of our nation. Furthermore, some of these people who are unable or unwilling to serve in the military, can also serve our country for two years in re-building our supply of commodities. God gave us the materials we need to come out of this deficit, And they include gold, silver, coal, natural gas, oil, wheat, corn, barley, and other materials. We could have individuals serve their two years working in facilities to find and extract or grow these items for our reserve. And, as the United States once again fills its asset base, then we can more comfortably know that we can afford the benefits that our citizens have come to love and enjoy. Finally, after they serve their two years, they would have paid the price for their social security, disability, unemployment, student loans, and other US benefits that people today take for granted. If they run away from their obligation, or don't finish their two year obligation, then they lose their right for these benefits.

The arguments will be out there. To begin with, is this the vision our forefathers had when the country was built?   George Washington was one of the first proponents of a national draft. He once said, "... it must be laid down as a primary position and the basis of our democratic) system, that every citizen who enjoys the protection of a free Government owes not only a proportion of his property, but even his personal service to the defense of it."   In fact, under George Washington, it was a requirement for white males to be part of the militia. [6]

---

[6] Most Americans don't realize what is at stake in the Global War on Terrorism (GWOT) with respect to American freedom and democracy. Just like the Cold War, the stakes in the Long War are high. It is imperative that the United States present a unified front to deal with GWOT issues. Its citizens are the backbone of this country. Leaders have a duty to make sure a solid foundation is laid for future generations of Americans by teaching citizens their roles and responsibilities in providing for the nation's defense. Building strong citizens by teaching them civic responsibility could be the greatest accomplishment of this generation. It is readily apparent that the GWOT is taking a toll on our military forces. The need to supplement our homeland security forces is real. Universal national service will provide the means for more citizens to shoulder their responsibilities on the home front as citizen soldiers. We must act now for the common good and a stronger nation. Research Paper from Marine Corps Command and Staff College, Title: National Service: Healing a Divided Nation through Servant Leadership, Written by: Schoonover, K. W., 19 February 2008.

Another bonus that the military gives an individual is the importance to be honest. Lie and get caught to a drill instructor, and your life becomes very difficult.

Our young people need to be taught how to be honest, because the world has taught them, especially through television, the opposite. Making young people serve two years in the military could help enforce some moral values that the world is just not teaching. The inability of man to say, "hey can you help me with this?" The military teaches young men how to ask for help, how to be humble for help, and how to be honest about not knowing something. We need a resurgence of honesty in this country.

Virginia Military Institute is one of the best schools I have ever heard of for stressing honesty. I had a friend who attended this school, and he told me how important the honor code was there. He explained to me the thought process that went behind answering a senior cadet about shining his shoes. He said, "you know, I would polish my boots. Then, a senior cadet would come in and ask, did I polish my boots?" The direct answer he said would be yes. However, if the boots were not shined to standard, he learned to ask himself "did I really shine my boots?" He said he had to watch all answers to questions to ensure his honesty from the inside of his soul. This is sort of like the response I anticipate Jesus will have when many go to heaven. There are so many individuals who have made the proverbial trek to the front of a church to be baptized on a Sunday morning, and have publically committed themselves to Christ. They have publically made a statement of faith, and in many times even been baptized. However, many of these people have not changed inwardly as Christ would have wanted. Christ was given for us to change the nasty, wicked, selfish inside of us that eludes every human being. When you are saved, if you live a life of Christ, you die to self and live for Christ, which is observable by serving others. Many saved people have made a statement that they believe, and many even believe that they are saved. However, many of these same individuals go on through life, and don't change anything. If you are saved, you will see the transformation. It may not all be at one time, but over a period of time you will change if you truly are a child of God. If you read the Bible and pray every day, your inner self will be changed.

While Thomas Jefferson was not for a national draft, he was for all citizens being ready to support their country if needed. Thomas Jefferson once said, "The Greeks and Romans had no standing armies, yet they defended themselves. Their system was to make every man a soldier and oblige him to repair to the standard of his country whenever that was reared. This made them

invincible; and the same remedy will make us so."[7]

So, let's say someone listened to me, and we

were able to formulate the militia that George

Washington envisioned for the country so many

years ago. What would that minuteman in the year

2012 and beyond look like? First of all, everyone

would be veterans of the military. Furthermore,

they would:

1.   Understands the role of the Bible as the

    ultimate training guide.

2.   Having already served at least two years in

---

[7] US Joint Forces Command (2008) has described the state failure of either Pakistan or Mexico as 'worst case scenarios' for US national security. Alarmed at the 'growing assault' on the Mexican state by the cartels, it warned that 'any descent by Mexico into chaos would demand an American response based on the serious implications for homeland security alone' (US Joint Forces Command 2008, 34, 38). In 2010 the Center for a New American Security (CNAS) issued a report arguing that 'criminal networks linking cartels and gangs are no longer simply a crime problem, but a threat that is metastasizing into a new form of widespread, networked criminal insurgency' that is no longer simply a problem for law enforcement but a 'strategic threat.' Article, The Everywhere War, by D. Gregory (2011), The Geographical Journal, 177: 238–250. doi: 10.1111/j.1475-4959.2011.00426.x

the military. (Understands military

courtesies and traditions)

3. Be trained in all weaponry, hunting, farming

and logistics.

4. Have his/her home stocked (food, water,

fuel, generator, etc.) and prepared for any

emergency.

5. Have weapons and ammunition stocked in

his home to repel any assault on

their home.

6. Trains his children how to hunt, fish, grow

food, and live off the land.

7. Has at least a 4 wheel drive truck and a 4

Wheeler.

8. Is active in his Christian church and

community.

9. Stands by his family and trains his children

to do right.

10.   Understands taking care of the

environment.

11.   Does unto others as he would have them

do unto themselves.

12.   Men and women would be actively

involved in their community watch and

political activities in their area.

The Role of Government

So, with that said, what should the role of

government be? Should our government mirror

Joseph's government, to where all individuals put

20% into the government during the good years, so that we are able to survive in the bad years? And, should this 20% come from all individuals or should it be pro-rated to where the top 10% pay the same amount as the median income earner. Well, in my eyes, 20% is 20%. However, most individuals will agree that government should be un-obtrusive, so as to allow every man and woman the freedom to pursue happiness. However, now that we have grown to where we are, what can we do to put ourselves back to where each individual contributes 20%? Let's look at some facts:

(1) People have become dependent on the government for taking care of them when they lose their jobs (Un-employment Benefits).

(2) People have become dependent on the government to ensure that their children are

properly Educated (Public Education).

(3) People have become dependent on the

government to ensure that they are covered

if they have a disability (Disability

Insurance).

(4) People have become dependent on the

government to ensure that they have an

income as they age (Social Security).

(5) People have become dependent on the

government to ensure that they have good

roads to drive on (Department of

Transportation).

(6) People have become dependent on the

government to ensure that they are safe

when they fly on an airplane FAA(Federal

Airlines Association).

(7) People have become dependent on the

government to ensure that the food that they eat is safe to eat. (Food and Safety Act).

(8) People have become dependent on the government to ensure that they can buy a home (Federal Housing Authority, Fannie Mae, Freddie Mac, VA, etc.).

(9) People have become dependent on the government to pay their medical bills when they do not have insurance (Medicare, Medicaid). [8]

---

[8] So it fascinated me to learn that in 30 states, (PDF of 30-state list) adult children are legally responsible, at least on paper, to pay for necessities like food, clothing, shelter and medical attention for indigent parents. These statutes, known as filial responsibility laws, are

modeled on the Elizabethan Poor Laws of 1601, which made blood relatives the primary source of support for family members, the elderly included. Public assistance was available only as a last resort. The American colonies had similar laws to England's — and they were enforced — until the advent of the New Deal, which created the Social Security system, intended to provide 45 percent of a worker's pre-retirement wages. That would keep mom and dad afloat in the good old days. Civil or criminal cases seeking assistance or reimbursement from adult children all but stopped. But, even more significant to the quiet passing of filial responsibility was the introduction of Medicaid, in 1965, a pillar of the Great Society, which had eligibility requirements that seemed at odds with the existing state laws, even though courts had upheld their

(10) People have become dependent on the

government when they cannot pay their bills

(Welfare and Bankruptcy Laws).

(11) People have become dependent on the

government when they get old and cannot

take care of themselves (Hospice and

Medicaid).

(12) People have become dependent on the

government when they cannot find a job (Jobs

Act, Employment Security Commission).

(13) Farmers have become dependent on

the government to pay for bad crops. (Farm

Subsidies, USDA).

(14) People have become dependent on the

government to pay for college (Stafford

---

constitutionality.   The New York Times, "Adult Children, Aging Parents and the Law," November 20, 2008.

Loans). Now, I am not complaining about any of these because they help stabilize our lives. And, I have gone to public schools to graduate from high school, obtained a VA loan to buy a house, gone to the VA Hospital, and utilized Tricare Insurance as I was employed by the US Military. These services are great.   These rights and benefits have been paid for by our ancestors, and were voted in by Senators such as Jessie Helms and Strom Thurman. However, there are many people who use these government programs and don't really need them.   And, there are people who make huge amounts of income and then lie about it to keep from paying taxes. And, I have seen recently some of these huge income earners who were last in trying to pay their 20% to the government during the good times, being the first in line to collect their unemployment and other benefits during the bad times. Is this right or selfish? Also, there are many people, including Military Personnel, State Employees, and others who worked 20 or more years for an agency, usually at a rate below the going average, with the promise of a retirement. This promise right now is getting ready to be broken, because senior leaders have not planned properly for people retiring. They have not taken the right amount and placed it to the side, to provide for these people when they retire. These leaders have not been truthful. Now, what is the solution, or is there one? We cannot treat Social Security, Federal and State Retirement, and other services as a Ponzi Scheme as others have insinuated. We have got to respect and pay for the obligations that are out in front of us. And, as a nation, we can. God gave us gold in the earth. We, as a country, need to start digging up this gold, and place it in our treasuries to help pay for that we are behind on. The solution that US Senators and Congressmen will want to come up with is that some people can keep their pensions and some cannot; usually around their votes and constituents.[9]   This will become

---

[9] Policymakers are working behind the scenes to come up with a way to let states declare bankruptcy and get out from under crushing debts, including the pensions they have promised to retired public workers. Unlike cities, the states are barred from seeking protection in federal bankruptcy court. Any effort to change that status would have to clear high constitutional hurdles because the states are considered sovereign. But proponents say some states are so burdened that the only feasible way out may be bankruptcy, giving Illinois, for example, the opportunity to do what General Motors did with the federal government's aid. Article titled "A Path Is Sought for States to Escape Their Debt Burdens," The New York Times, January 20, 2011, by Mary Williams Walsh

increasingly unfair, especially to the

thousands of retired Military Service Members

who expect and depend on their retirement

benefits and Tricare Health Insurance. After all,

these are the men and women who fought for the

rest of us to be able to sit in our recliner, drink our

Pepsi Colas, and watch the evening news. You

know, we promised these people these pensions.

And now, we have screwed the pooch and have no

solution on how to pay for them. What was the

plan up front, and how did we mess this up so

bad? How did we pay these leaders so much

money to ensure that things were taken care of,

just to get where we are today trying to figure out

how to pay for it? It is such a tragedy. But, no

matter what, we can recover. Let's look at the

worst case scenario. The United States and all the

states therein go bankrupt. (I will look at a second

option in a few pages). There is no Universal

Healthcare. China, our largest creditor, actually

by default becomes the owner of much of the

Federal Land throughout the United States,

and also the owner of Federal Pension funds.

People who are on retirement from the military,

Federal, State and Local governments, lose

their pensions, and have to go back to work or are

offered new positions in the military or elsewhere.

A mandatory Federal retirement age of 60 is

removed from the military. People are allowed and

encouraged to work until they are no longer able to

get up and go to work. Money from other pension

accounts are also frozen, until International

Bankruptcy Courts are able to decide who gets

what money. People and institutions are pissed,

angry, and sullen but they learn to survive again.

I love the United States of America, and the

God Fearing and hard-working people therein.

However, we may need to take a step back and
reset our country from the mistakes that have been

made. And, these are some tough choices.

However, as we often do, we learn from our

past mistakes. We cannot write checks for more

than we have in our checking account. Some

of the positive items that would come out of us

starting over again include:

- The United States goes back to backing

  all currency with gold in reserves. [10]

---

[10] Among the chief advocates of a return to the full gold standard for both the
U.S. and European nations are French Economic Adviser Jacques Rueff, the
architect of France's successful financial-austerity program, and Philip Cortney,
president of Coty, Inc. and chairman of the U.S. Council of the International Chamber of
Commerce. They, like the rest of a small but dedicated group of economists, believe that the
gold standard is the only answer to the world's present monetary problems, such as inflation
and a concentration of capital. They believe that a return to the rigid fiscal discipline of the
gold standard would act as a brake on inflation by preventing governments from
overspending, head off world recessions by doing away with the excesses that lead to them.
A full gold standard, as they see it, would also put a damper on sudden expansions of credit
not backed by gold, help stabilize prices, and step up the flow of capital—and thus

- The United States government has to formulate a yearly budget within the   taxes they receive, and work within it.

- Individuals become dependent on families to take care of one another. The family unit becomes stronger, and is rebuilt.

- The Federal Government once again understands that it is small business, construction, trade, farming, and Wall Street that drives the economy; not the government driving the economy.   The government may regulate and ensure ethics, but we cannot all work for the government and expect a sound financial

---

international trade—by making all currencies freely convertible into gold. Time Magazine Article, Monday October 12, 1959, The Gold Standard: Should the US Go Back to It?

government. This finally becomes apparent as money runs out of the Federal Government, at the same time the Federal Government is trying to give unemployed men and women jobs.

- The Church becomes a 2nd home for many people.   More people become saved and the understanding that we are completely dependent on God for all becomes paramount. The church once again becomes the storehouse for those in need, as Franklin Graham has foreseen with Operation Blessing.
- The US Government sells a lot of land it does not really need, including about 36% of Nevada. It also sells buildings, vehicles, etc.
- People start small businesses at a rate

faster than ever before. We as a nation once again become a manufacturing country. Mill houses and factory housing becomes available. We once again become the furniture manufacturing capital of the world. People start working for minimum wage again instead of waiting for an above minimum wage welfare check.

- People become willing to work for companies for a reasonable wage. Companies move back into America from overseas.
- A focus on the Constitution is once again reborn.
- After about 5 years, the ratings from Moody's, etc. will again give the US an AAA rating again.

- The US Military creates a Financial Justification Branch that is designed to pay for our own invasions and Wars. IE: The next invasion (Pakistan, North Korea, Somalia, Iran etc.) is paid for by obtained resources from the country we invade. As Sun Tzu stated in The Art of War, "By taking equipment from your own country but feeding off the enemy, you can be sufficient in both arms and provisions. When a country is impoverished by military operations, it is because of transporting supplies to a distant place. Transport supplies to a distant place, and the populace will be impoverished. Those who are near the army sell at high prices. Because of high prices, the wealth of the common people is exhausted." Sun Tzu,

The Art of War, On Doing battle.

The second option that I would

Recommend, but it would take giving

A little from all of us, is to keep taxes at their

same levels, but to decrease paid out Federal,

State and Local Benefits from pension plans,

Social Security, Disability, Welfare and all other

Such subsidies to 78% of their current values.

This includes also the paycheck of the current and

Future Federal, State and Local government

Employee. So, if I am now a Police Officer and I

Now take home $1,000 from the city of

Fayetteville, NC now every two weeks, my

paycheck will be reduced to $780 every two weeks.

This will be a belt tightening for all, but it would

Make it to where we all could keep all the services,

benefits and pensions that we have for all. Now,

will this make people angry? Yes. But, it is better to keep 78% of something than to get 0% when it is all lost. And, if we are going to take this second option, we need to all come together today and take it. No going into the streets of Oakland, California and protesting because it is not fair. No Trying to form militias to reform the government. Just an understanding on all levels that we made mistakes trying to help others in the past, we have been burnt by it, and we need to self-correct from our errors. The 78% option keeps the jobs available for our employees, and the pensions (although at a reduced level) for everyone. I Personally would like to see option (2) as it would Ensure we all have jobs and that there is little Change. And, my father and mother can still Receive the benefits from Social Security and Medicare that they need, although perhaps at a reduced level. And, we don't default, give up land, or find ourselves with an increased amount of homeless people.

As I said, I like plan (2), to reduce pay outs to 78% of current levels to ensure everything stays the same. However, there will be a lot of people up in arms I am sure. The "entitled people" will not want to give up anything, to the point that they will keep raising taxes and benefits to the point the country collapses and our only option is option (1). The entitled people are the ones that frustrate me the most , because they are not in America to Work hard and make a better future for themselves and their children. They exist in America as an anchor, weighing down the wealth and productivity of those willing to work. Some of these "entitled people" are not even willing to take a test to see if they have illegal drugs in their system prior to receiving welfare. So, we pay for some "entitled" people to actually sit around and smoke marijuana and crack.

Now, don't get me wrong; I am not completely against Socialistic programs, but I am against certain people getting huge amounts of Disability payments while they work a private job, while others who are truly injured have to fight to get Federal Disability. Or, it is not fair for a single mother of four to work three jobs to make ends meet, and another single mother to plan to have an additional child for an additional $158 (or whatever dollar amount it is) a month from Welfare. Also, there are people who need and deserve VA Disability Payments. These people have fought wars and spent time away from families for our country and protecting the liberties and freedoms of others, and then they cannot get

VA Disability. This is the one of the most shameful

arguments of why we need to revamp our system.

Our Veterans deserve so much more than that.

Rome used to give its returning Veterans land for

service in War. [11]   What do our Veterans get?

Many are homeless. Many have psychological

problems that they cannot recover from (PTSD,

Schizophrenia, Depression, etc.).[12] In fact last

---

[11]The Roman army (*exercitus*) did not start out as the superlative fighting machine that came to dominate Europe to the Rhine, parts of Asia, and Africa. It began like the part-time Greek army, with farmers returning to their fields after a quick summer campaign. Then it changed into a professional organization with long terms of service far from home. The Roman general and 7-time consul Marius is considered responsible for the change of the Roman army into its professional form. He gave the poorest classes in Rome the opportunity to be career military, gave land to veterans, and changed the composition of the legion. **Article Titled: The Roman Army of the Roman Republic, by N. S. Gill, Author, www.about.com**

[12]
Nearly a third of veterans returning from Iraq and Afghanistan who received care from Veterans Affairs between 2001 and 2005 were diagnosed with mental health or psychosocial ills, a study published Monday has concluded. The study was published in the March 12 issue of Archives of Internal Medicine and carried out by researchers at the University of California, San Francisco and the San Francisco VA Medical Center. They looked at data from 103,788 veterans; about

week, while I was on routine patrol as a Police

Officer, an Army Staff Sergeant shot a high

powered rifle at me, and several people are stating

this is because he had PTSD. I do not know. A

woman who wrote in the Paper an editorial

response stated that they should not be

too hard on the guy because he may have had

PTSD. Many Veterans return and

become dependent on alcohol, drugs, and high

risk lifestyles. There is a cost for being a soldier in

the United States Military, that for many will cost

them their lives. In fact, there are probably more

soldiers who are killing themselves with high risk

lifestyles after returning from a War Zone than that

---

13 percent of them women, 54 percent under age 30, nearly a third minorities and nearly half veterans of the National Guard or Reserves. Article titled Thousands of Veterans Return with Mental Illness, March 12,2007, www.CNN.com,

actually die in a War Zone. I know when I returned from Iraq during my first deployment, we had a couple of soldiers get killed on a motorcycle, suicides, and other deaths. I recently went to the Funeral of a soldier I deployed with who killed herself for unknown reasons. Serving in a War Zone has effects on people that often go undiagnosed until it is too late. This soldier was a single mother of a 17 year old son, who had survived being in a vehicle hit by an IED, and came back to America and became so depressed that she took it upon herself to kill herself.   And, recently while working my shift as a Police Officer, I came across a soldier who was under the influence of "bath salts." I had never even heard of such. There were several soldiers from his unit who were already out with him, and we tried to talk him into walking with us to our car so we could take him to get help. But, he could not even recognize who we were. He kept talking about someone coming to get him, and I wound up having to put him in handcuffs to take him to Fort Bragg, NC to get psychological treatment. He was a soldier attached to a Special Forces unit, so I am sure he was fairly squared away. But, his lifestyle was atrocious. Another Special Forces soldier we responded to recently was under suspicion of a crime, and placed a knife in his own throat and jaggedly cut back and forth from the back to the front.   He acted like it did not even hurt.

I have lived over two years in Iraq. The first time was not so bad. I was in the Diyala

Province near Iran and it was overall peaceful and tranquil, except for the occasional RPG or other munitions lobbed at us. Don't get me wrong, there were several people killed from my Brigade, but overall it was not that bad. The second time I was over there, I lived in Baghdad on FOB Liberty, and the wind and sand blew all year. I had never seen such sand storms and dust as I saw there. I have sinus problems today that I know are from breathing in the sand and dust in that area, and don't forget all the munitions we blew up in the sand that we all probably breathed in also. Who knows the long term effects of breathing in the metal and depleted uranium still in the dust from this war. It is stated that depleted uranium stays in the environment for at least 21 years.

I do yard work and other small jobs on the side to help support my family. Recently, I worked on cutting weeds, bushes and other debris on a hill. It took two days to complete. I had cut this same hill the previous year. The hill was full of vines, trees, and trash. When I finished the hill last year, it was clean and had no growth. I kept thinking, if they would just do a little bit of work to keep this hill mowed or cleared it would be so much easier to keep up with. However, the Church just leaves it alone all year till the Fall, when I go out there and clean it. This growth is identical to how the VA treats our soldiers. They do not want to treat or give benefits to Veterans benefits until they are in really bad shape. And then, suddenly, after they have shot someone or at someone, they bring them in and treat them like they should have been treated in the first place. Then, once they are treated, they forget about them until they have the next episode, as the church forgets the weeds on the hill. That is such a shame, especially for the ones who really have bad physical and mental scars and injuries from war.

So, why is this so important? Why should we do the right thing? Well, let me go over a couple of more Items and then we will get into the importance of doing the right thing.

The first thing to discuss is ethics. What is ethics? Ethics is basically telling the difference between right and wrong, justice, etc. America is designed on that function:

good. Nothing works right in America when we place evil first. Our understanding between good and evil is basically as well founded as Napoleon's, as he believed the moral is to the physical, as 3:1. Our forefathers believed this also. We place trust in our banking institutions, in the day care that we put our children in, in our schools, in our schools that our teachers are teaching our children correctly. We have to trust one another, as well as our businesses and our government.

We are at war. When we do that which is right, God is with us and will bless us and will continue to be with us. Napoleon once said, the moral is to the physical as 3:1. That means we can win wars when we are the moral majority. But, when we become as evil as our enemy, then he cannot stand to look at us. We are at war with the Muslims and will continue to be at war with them because they see us as infidels. It is only through prayer, fasting, and righteous living that we will continue to be safe from them.

After 911, we begin to see how important the safety and security of our nation is. Many additional American's fell to their knees, and our nation began to rebuild on some of our downfalls. We invaded Iraq, and toppled Saddam. We set up bases in the Middle East to fight terrorists on their own ground, and we became aggressive on helping other countries build democratic governments. However, about 2006, we started forgetting. By 2008, the country became forgetful of how important it is to fight for our country. The additional prayers and support for our troops to fight for our future, was forgotten and replaced by episodes of Desperate Housewives, The Sopranos, and Survivor. We simply forgot that by which was right, and the direction we needed to take for our security of our nation. Once again, our nation was built on Christian values and doing that which was right, not laziness....not passiveness. But, that is where we went. By 2008, more people once again were interested in movies like "The

Hangover" and other Hollywood moral busters, than

anything focusing on the need to support our troops. Yet,

 the troops were still in Afghanistan, Iraq, and starting

movements toward injustices in Africa.

In 2008, we elected Congressmen and Senators that

voted to allow gays to serve openly in the military.   We

did not think that it matters that most service men and

women are Christians and want to do the right thing.   We

did not think that the largest security that we have in this

nation and as a soldier is from God.   God has protected

our country and our soldiers for so many years. We forgot

Sodom and Gomorrah, and other places in the Bible where

God said it is an abomination for a man to lie with a man

as a woman, or that is immoral for a woman to work that

by which is unnatural with another woman. But, we have

supported it.

One of the newest shows on television in 2011 is

"skins" a show on MTV showing 16 year olds and below having sex, smoking marijuana and doing drugs. The Producers say that they are just showing the world what is real throughout America. However, what about the child that did not know others acted like that until they saw it on MTV. What about a Muslim girl, taught by her parents to stay covered to keep others from sinning. At this point, I have to say we are losing moral ground. Freedom of thought, actions, movement, careers......these were 1st Amendment rights that our forefathers believed in..... . Freedom to put naked teenagers on television; was this thought of by the writers of the Constitution?

Our greatest moral guide for what is right and wrong is the Bible. We keep advancing as a society, and we believe that man is becoming smarter than God and the Bible. (Remember what happened at Babylon when man became Capable of doing everything?) We keep advancing by cloning sheep and humans, making hybrid seeds, mixing breeds of animals, and even using chemicals instead of food to grow animals and humans.

American's love insurance. They want to pay low premiums, but they want their insurance to pay claims if their home is destroyed, if their car is damaged, if they lose everything…they want repayment. Like I said, they want the lowest price though.

We believe we know and understand everything. Many people now believe that they are the creator, and that man is in charge. So many people in Hollywood especially want American's to forget the miracle of life, blood, oxygen, or clean drinking water.

We don't believe we would ever be destroyed. We don't believe that we as Americans can be hurt. But the truth is, right now somewhere there are human beings plotting to kill you. Maybe not you personally, but you and thousands of other American's. The reason is that we are not like them. They are Muslim. We are most likely not.

What if we were wrong. What if we cancelled our Insurance policy with God. What if we all turned our backs on God, as well as what is right, and he suddenly came back as the Bible says he will. Based off Revelations, and I believe in the Pre-Millennial Theory, then we Christians will be taken out of play early. However, would everyone else still be alright? Would those not taken still be blessed and able to function as a nation. Would we still have satellite telephones, MTV, Google, microwave dinners, Denny's? Would everyone left back on earth still be ok? Well, the Bible says initially everyone will be alright. Those who align with the new government and get their chip or 666 marks as others want. But, what if God completely turned his back on us. What if he forgot about the seasons of the year, about the rain for the crops, about keeping the sea at the right level, about maintaining an appropriate temperature for mankind to live in, about providing clean water, shelter, food. What if he just vanished, as so many of his believers have Don? What if he left man alone in 2012 or beyond, especially after the rapture? Have we put our 20% away to the government for them to take care of us? Have we elected the right people into positions of authority who will take care of us?

Or, could we as humans just vanish. Could man destroy himself as quickly as God made him? Could we be our own worst enemy. Why would it be so hard and so bad for us to live lives worthy of God's blessing. And for those who don't believe, why don't they just take the insurance for insurance sake, just in case they need it. Why can we as a society not do this? (Asking Jesus to come into your life and forgive you of your sins is the greatest insurance policy ever given.) And then turning to God and the Bible and learning to live a life worthy to him.

We have to look. We as human beings will always be sinners. We have to be entertained. If it is in front of us, we can't help but look. Remember when Lot was leaving Sodom and Gomorrah. God told Lot not to look back, and he did not and survived. But Sarah looked, and was turned into ashes. I personally have had a lot of failures and problems in my past, and I keep thinking of them often in life. And, I like to look in the past at my failures, especially when I feel I suck at something or have lost confidence. However, we should learn from our mistakes…but we have to learn to let go and to forgive the hardest person to forgive….ourselves. And, I am the worlds worst. God has forgiven me for my sins…yet they come back into my mind when I am feeling the worst.

What I am asking of you today is to take some free insurance. To commit your life to the principles that were given in the Old Testament of the Bible , and by Jesus when he said "do unto others as you would have them do unto you." And to "love thy neighbor as thyself." It is not that much to ask. You; as a great leader, you know you can do that. You can do what is right. You can vote your conscience. You can help weed out corruption, pride, vanity , deception, prejudice, hate, adultery. You can be productive and work hard and help this Economy of ours to survive again. You can do this. It is not up to our government to do this for us. It is up to you. You can be a better Christian, husband/wife, father/mother, or provider.

You can do these things. Not on your own, but with God. For when Egypt was about to be devastated with 7 years of famine after 7 years of plenty, God already had given the country a great leader. Joseph. He stored the grain, and helped a nation of people survive. And, God will provide for us another great leader when the time is right.

You see, you need to be the person doing that by which is right, so that you can more fully bless others. We need God filled men that are capable of making good decisions. The below is a decision matrix. While it does not always give the best answer, it does give a great look at why a decision should be made. Let's look at a simple decision: where to go on Vacation (1 is best and 4 is worst).

Vacation Choices	Most memorable for my family.	Fits best within my budget.	Easiest to plan.	Will give an educational benefit for my children.	Total
Myrtle Beach	3	1	1	4	9
Banner Elk, NC	4	2	2	3	11
Cruise	2	3	3	2	10
Hawaii	1	4	4	1	10

So, based off the choices of the decision matrix, Myrtle Beach would be the best place for me to take my family. But, is this the best choice. The next step is something radical, and something that 90% of you are going to think is crazy but I want you to try it next time on a big decision anyway. You have now looked at the options, you have now seemingly made a decision off a decision matrix of what is seemingly best. Now, I want you to wake up on a morning when you are not stressed to get to work or somewhere else, close your closet door, get on your knees, and pray for each one. See as you pray and ask God for his input what he says. It will be a gentle nudge, but you will get the nudge. And , when you do, go firmly and confidently in that direction. Trust God. That is best way to make an ethical decision. You have the 100% solution in your head and body to make good decisions.

Many of you were already making great decisions in line with the will of God. But, some of you may only make ½ way thought through decisions.   You have the power to change. You can take the free insurance policy that is given and insure your life, or you can continue to ignore it, as the people of Babylon, Sodom and Gomorrah, Rome, Germany and other countries have.

However, there have been other great nations before us that believed that they were smarter than God. There have been leaders that believed that they controlled the destinies of Their countries, and not God.   There have been countries before that believed that they were invincible.

Our forefathers wanted so much more than to grow to a point, and then to vanish because we lost our way. To wander through the wilderness for so many years, and then to be blessed with the land of milk and honey, only to have it taken away because Hollywood has warped our minds into believing that is the way everyone acts. According to Hollywood, you are wrong not to accept homosexuals as a normal pattern of life . You are a cook or crazy if you go to church and worship God. Your family is so backward if the mother and father stays through life as a monogamous couple. No one does that any more. In fact, it is more normal for a husband and wife to be divorced today in many cases than it is to remain married. Well, I as well as many others are tired of it.

There is a right and there is a wrong and we have to begin to know this as a man and as a government so we can save ourselves. You see, we are our own worst enemy. If you don't believe me, then I would like for you to pay attention to the following: right now as you sit and read this, scientists are developing weapons capable of destroying the world. Oh, they are not producing them with that intention. But, there are 2nd and 3rd and 4th order effects to many of these experiments. (39)

An example of this is a program funded by the United States Navy and Army for research into ELF Wave

Technology bouncing off the Ionosphere. (There are also open programs also funded by the European Community and Russia, and probably secret programs funded by North Korea, Iran, and Venezuela). The High Frequency Active Aural Research Program (HAARP) was Created to "increase knowledge of the physical and Electrical properties of the Earth's ionosphere, which can affect our military and civilian communication and navigation systems," according to HAARP's official website. All of the research, scientists, universities, and reasoning look legitimate, and I completely trust our government as a whole. What I do question is the lone person who does not have the correct check and balances.

As a background to this, there have been an increase in tropical storms, drought, polar ice caps melting, and other weather related phenomena over the last few years; and the frequency of such disasters seem to be increasing. Storms such as Hurricane Katrina and Irene, earthquakes in Haiti and Japan, unexplained mass bird and fish death, burning

fires and drought throughout Texas, and other disasters

have become common. While many of these weather

changes can be attributed to the changing of the earths

natural surface and weather systems, many ecologists have

become concerned that we (human beings) have done this

to ourselves. One specific concern that many government

leaders, writers, and researchers have raised is that the

increasing use of both government and private companies

performing weather modification (whether it is intended or

not) is causing the earth's natural rhythm to become

skewed. HAARP on its own website discusses that it

performs Ionosphere Heating. HAARP states that this

heating affects only the Rarefied Region of the Earths

Ionosphere, about 70km above the earth's surface, thus

not affecting the weather. However, many government

leaders do not believe that the research is conclusive. The

main reason for this disbelief is that weather modification

is real, has been in existence in one form or another since at least 1947, and is continuing to become more advanced. The students and scientists who perform these Ionosphere Heating experiments are from major Universities including Stanford and MIT, as well as from the US Navy and the US Air Force.

The Ionosphere consists of the top layer of the earths atmosphere from 30 miles to 600 miles above the earths surface. It is important to life forms, because it serves as a skin like layer to the earth, protecting the earth from incoming cosmic radiation.   Within the ionosphere region, there are invisible layers of ions and electrons, which actually form this skin.   The temperature within the ionosphere varies from -99.4 degrees Fahrenheit to 440.6 degrees Fahrenheit.   According to the National Earth Science Teachers Association, the main component that creates this layer is the sun's ultraviolet light, which helps to ionize molecules and atoms in the upper atmosphere of the earth, thus protecting life forms from radiation and other dangerous rays from the sun. The sun has flares which produce ultraviolet, x-ray, and gamma ray photons, as well as geo-magnetically induced currents. (26) Radiation arrives on the earth approximately eight minutes after sun flare ups, and it actually causes the ionosphere to thicken. This thickening is actually called plasma. When the sun is increasingly active, the ionosphere becomes thicker, in order to reflect these flare ups from affecting temperature on the earths surface. Thus, the ionosphere acts as a natural skin for the earth, to protect it from damage from outer space.

There are many reasons for conducting research inside of the Ionosphere region of the atmosphere. However, one of the most important reasons is due to its application with worldwide communications. In 1901, Guglielmi Marconi discovered that radio waves would bounce off the Ionosphere region instead of heading straight into outer space as previously believed. Thus, his research helped to

discover worldwide communication techniques, for
telephones and radios. Furthermore, satellites normally
orbit the earth within or below the ionosphere region to
transmit radio signals and GPS signals throughout the
earth. Within the ionosphere, are three layers, in differing
altitudes, known as the D (70-110km), E (110km-250km),
and F (250+ km) layers, and whose position

the altitude of the layers of the ionosphere change
constantly. The "E" layer and "F" Layer reflect radio
waves. The lowest level, known as the "D" level, absorbs
the waves. These differing layers of the ionosphere absorbs
or reflects radio waves, and has effects on earth to earth
transmissions, and signaling to and from satellite.

Explanation of the High Frequency Active Auroral Research Program

The HAARP facility is a world-class ionosphere
research facility located about 8 miles North of Gakona,
Alaska. Most research and scholarly publications

regarding The HAARP program, state that it was designed to increase "knowledge of the physical and electrical properties of the Earth's ionosphere which can affect our military and civilian communication and navigation systems." Basically it is conducting research on the different layers of the ionosphere listed above. The major contractor that was involved in the construction of the facility is BAE Systems, Advance Technology (BAE/AT), and they completed construction on the facility in 2007. A site in Alaska was chosen for several reasons, including that Alaska is the only state in the auroral (or polar) region depending on how active the sun is at any given time and day. The facility being in the auroral region allows for varying ranges of ionosphere conditions to study. An additional reason the HAARP facility was placed in Alaska is that it controls a HF transmitter, as well as other scientific instruments, that requires a quiet, electromagnetic location.

One primary technology enhancement of HAARP is the

study of communication by the Navy with underwater submarines utilizing the ionosphere. Research has shown that the degree to which a signal is received and transmitted, depends on its frequency. The lower the frequency, the more deeply a signal can be received in sea water. In the past, communications with submarines have been difficult due to the density of salt water.

Furthermore, for a submarine to receive a conventional radio transmission, a submarine must travel at slow speeds and be near the surface of the water, which makes it susceptible to enemy detection. Frequencies in the ELF range, however, can be transmitted considerably deeper, and provide a link between Commanders and their Submarines. [13]

---

[13] ELF was accidentally detected in World War I when the Germans noticed a very low frequency noise in the ground which had a strong resonance at 7 Hz. In 1952 a German scientist, W.O. Schuman pointed out the existence of a cavity between the earth and the ionosphere that has a fundamental resonant frequency of about 7hz. A radio wave having the same frequency can be broadcast into this cavity and will travel around the world at the speed of light. Other scientists soon followed suit and discovered that other frequencies below 100hz do not fade out. These discoveries helped to create the ELF Theory. ELF was accidentally detected in World War I when the Germans noticed a very low frequency noise in the ground which had a strong resonance at 7 Hz. In 1952 a German scientist, W.O. Schuman pointed out the existence of a cavity between the earth and the ionosphere that has a fundamental resonant frequency of about 7hz. A

The importance of Ionosphere research, and utilization of ELF range transmissions, is important to military operations. Furthermore, it is important for Commanders to be able to communicate effectively with their troops throughout the world, and in a secured setting.

The Problem

We have previously discussed that ionosphere research is necessary and effective. We have discussed that the High Frequency Active Aural Research Program (HAARP) facility is one of the leading places for research regarding ELF Transmissions, and benefits both the United States Air Force and United States Navy.

However, some problems begin with the internet, and its ease of posting information throughout the world. One only has to Google the High Frequency Active Aural

---

radio wave having the same frequency can be broadcast into this cavity and will travel around the world at the speed of light. Other scientists soon followed suit and discovered that other frequencies below 100hz do not fade out. These discoveries helped to create the ELF Theory. The ELF Odyssey, L.W. Klessig and V.L. Strite, Westview Press, 1980.

Research Program (HAARP) to receive thousands of

postings regarding HAARP, and its alleged research that is

affecting the earth and its ecosystems. Throughout the

internet, it is alleged that the use of Ionosphere Heating, as

well as the use of these ELF signals, affects the weather
and

causes earthquakes. This 2nd order effect is from the

 byproduct of the transmissions of these low frequency

waves. There are articles, books, blogs, and other

information throughout the Internet that state that HAARP

has done everything from create Hurricane Katrina,

earthquakes in Haiti, China, and New Zealand, the

Earthquake and Tsunami in Japan, a drought in the United

Kingdom, and birds and fish dying throughout the world.

There are reports throughout the internet on the Air Force

and its desire to control the weather by 2025. [14]   With the

---

[14] It could have offensive and defensive applications and even be used for
deterrence purposes. The ability to generate precipitation, fog, and storms on
earth or to modify space weather…and the production of artificial weather all
are a part of an integrated set of technologies which can provide substantial
increase in US, or degraded capability in an adversary, to achieve global

current increase in weather systems, which include

earthquakes, one begins to wonder if maybe there is some

truth to these allegations. (40) And, if there is even a half

truth, then shouldn't this information be published for
the public?

On 10 August 2000, the Interfax News reported that

"The Russian State Dumas has expressed concern about the

USA's program to develop a qualitatively new type of

weapon. The article states that "the USA plans to carry

out large-scale scientific experiments under the HAARP

program, not controlled by the global community, that

will create weapons capable of breaking radio

communication lines and equipment installed on spaceships

and rockets, provoke serious accidents in electricity

networks and in oil and gas pipelines, and have a negative

impact on the mental health of people populating entire

---

awareness, reach and power." Air University of the US Air Force, AF 2025
Final Report, http://www.au.af.mil/au/2025/

regions," the deputies said. They demanded that an international ban is put on such large-scale geophysical experiments.

On 21 January 2010, Andrew Moran, a writer for The Digital Journal, wrote that "media reports claim Chavez's state mouthpiece ViVe TV is blaming the US for causing the 7.0 magnitude earthquake in Haiti as part of testing a tectonic weapon that can cause eco-type disasters, according to Russia Today. Fox News states that the information was apparently gathered by Russia's north Fleet. The Latin American leader added that the US should stop playing God." The TV report said these weapon earthquakes would eventually be used against Iran, for them to be taken over by the US military.

On 28 September 2010, Wall Street Journal Writer Brett Stephens wrote an article discussing an interview that he had with the President of Iran. In it President Ahmadinejad discusses his belief that "the recent floods in

Pakistan are acts neither of God nor of nature.

Rather, they are the result of a secret US military project

called HAARP, based out of Fairbanks,

Alaska, which controls the weather by sending

electromagnetic waves into the upper atmosphere.

HAARP may also be responsible for the recent spate of

tsunamis and earthquakes." (41)

These are just a couple of examples of the allegations

that are being posted against HAARP and its intentions.

Furthermore, if the HAARP program is actually research

for a weapon system, then Russia will also have this

weapon system, as well as the European Community as

they all are competing with the United States on ELF

Waves and Ionosphere Research. So, while I keep

speaking about the HAARP Facility in the US, I could also

be speaking about Russia and the European Communities

Ionosphere Project also. So, while I am speaking about the

US on this, know that we do need to have a facility to learn

To counter what may be coming our way.

Discussion

(1)Can ELF Waves Cause an earthquake?

Yes, Earthquakes (that have a Richter scale of 6 or higher)

begin when the layers of the Earth's crust fracture as

stress builds along the fault lines. When the shifting

begins, the bedrock creates ELF Magnetic Waves. This

is sort of like how a glass shatters or moves across a table

with deep base music or woofers. HAARP is the most

powerful Ionosphere Heating Facility in the World. ELF

waves can create an earthquake.[15] Have you ever

---

[15] HAARP and other, similar installations in Russia near Nizhni Novgorod – in which the US have participated – can also emit pulsating, extremely low frequencies as waves (ELF), which are aimed deep into the Earth. These waves are capable of tearing apart the precariously balanced tectonic plates of the Earth"s crust. The investigations into the subterranean world that thus become possible are also called "deep earth-" or "earth-penetrating tomography". According to Bertell, however, we know very little indeed about the interplay of tectonic plates, volcanoes and the Earth"s molten core. For example, a Soviet experiment in the ionosphere was conducted shortly before an earthquake in China 1967, which claimed 650,000 lives. In the US, ELF-waves were detected just before the 1989 earthquake in San Francisco, and similar unnatural and inexplicable waves appeared before the earthquakes in Japan in 1989, as well as the one in Los Angeles in 1994. One thing that is certain, as Bertell demonstrates, is that the global incidence of earthquakes is more than twice as high since the military began experiments affecting the atmosphere and the Earth itself. But there is more evidence that something unusual is afoot. **Werlhof, Claudia** Call for a "Planetary Movement for

taken a tuning fork and shaken a glass? Now, take this amount of interference and multiply it times 1,000(+), and you will discover that This is the capabilities that ELF waves can have if employed improperly. Low Frequency ELF waves can shatter a building and make it collapse. They can shake rock formations and make them move. Therefore, the HAARP Facility, as well as other Ionosphere Heating facilities, can create an earthquake if the waves are not precisely transmitted from individuals with expert training, or if the ELF Waves hit a fault line at the right frequency and timing. Another example of this is when when you have been sitting in your house and seen a glass or other item shake and move when a jet flew over? This is the same concept, except the sound waves are being produced at a larger level, and they are able to move tectonic plates. (42)

Mother Earth," International Goddess-Conference, "Politics and Spirituality," Castle Hambach, Germany 29 May 2010.

(2) Can ELF Waves Affect the Weather?

Yes, Nikola Tesla, a Russian Scientist who conducted experiments during the early 1900's, recorded the effects that "harmonious radio frequencies make when they impact air molecules. The molecules become excited and give off negatively charged electrons which readily combine with hydrogen and oxygen to produce water molecules." The HAARP Facility conducts research on the Ionosphere and deals with ELF Waves. Nikola Tesla in the early 1900's, as well as other scientists since, have shown that ELF Waves can create weather systems. (11) This is not to say that HAARP has ever created a weather system; just that it has the potential to do so.

(3) Are other facilities conducting Ionosphere Research?

Yes, There are several Ionospheres Heating Facilities throughout the world, operated by the United States, Russia, and a European facility. The High Power Auroral

Stimulation (HIPAS) facility is located approximately 30

miles Northeast of Fairbanks, Alaska. The Arecibo

Observatory, also called the National Astronomy and

Ionosphere Center (NAIC), is located near Arecibo, Puerto

Rico. The Sure Ionosphere Heating Facility is located near

the town of Vasilsursk, Russia. The European Incoherent

SCATter (EISCAT) is defined as a scientific and

educational organization which was designed to conduct

high attitude upper atmosphere research by the Incoherent

Scatter technique. The EISCAT Scientific Association is

governed by a council with members from Germany,

France, Japan, Norway, Sweden, and the United Kingdom.

So, the United States, Russia, and the European

Community are all competing to become experts on

Ionosphere Research, and ELF Wave technology. And,

these are the ones we know of. Iran and other countries secretly conduct research so that it is not open knowledge. Is Iran right now researching a Plan to destroy the United States with earthquake technology?

(4) Is there United Nations oversight to facilities conducting Ionosphere Research?   No, Oversight was discussed but not implemented at the Framework Convention on Climate Change (UNFCCC) signed at the 1992 Earth Summit in Rio de Janeiro, where the responsibilities for oversight on the facilities were given back to the states. Specifically it addressed that "states have, in accordance with the Charter of the United Nations and the principles of international law, the responsibility to ensure that activities within their jurisdiction or control do not cause damage to the environment of other states or areas beyond the limits of national jurisdiction."

(5) Should we hide the technology we are gaining from

HAARP Research, or should we openly

publish it?   We should openly publish it. In April 2000,

LTCOL Beth Kaspar, USAF submitted a Research Report

basically stating that the world is becoming transparent,

and the military has gotten to become capable of fighting

wars knowing that information is flowing rapidly. Her

thesis was that "the US military must consciously prepare

itself to fight in information transparent world created by

globalization. The worldwide explosion in the quantity and

quality of information and products available to the general

public user, the ready accessibility to the information, and

the affordability in acquiring any desired data or product

are creating a transparent world at an alarming rate. In the

future, anyone can affordably keep tabs on the actions of

everyone else.   Hence, the US military must consciously

begin to investigate ways to maintain its military advantage

in this rapidly evolving transparent world. It must

minimize the impact transparency has on how we will fight

wars and conduct contingency actions." (21)

Transparency regarding HAARP and the results it has had on weather modification should be openly published. There have been thousands of experiments with differing types of methods to change the weather. There is no reason why two of the same experiments should be attempted, especially with something as sensitive as weather. For example, on 13 October 1947, the United States Military and General Electric, during Project Cirrus, dropped 80 kg of dry ice into a hurricane which was formed in the Atlantic Ocean. This hurricane was safely off the Eastern Coast of the United States. After they did this, the hurricane allegedly changed direction, and went toward Georgia, where it did extensive damage. Whereas one would expect that this research would be published openly, so future scientists would know the results, attorneys for General Electric reviewed and censored the work of Dr. Irwin Langmuir. However, in his Collected Works from 1952, he published that "there was approximately a 99% probability that this hurricane's change of direction was the direct result of the cloud seeding."[16]

Significance of the Study

The atmosphere is made up of several layers, including the troposphere, stratosphere, mesosphere, ionosphere, and exosphere. These layers basically help to hold in a series of gasses, including water vapor, carbon dioxide, methane, nitrous oxide, and others. These gasses help to keep in heat, which is radiated back to warm the surface of the

---

[16] Dr. Vonnegut, appearing in 1952 before a U.S. Senate committee that was considering legislation on weather modification, said: Theory has predicted and experiments are confirming the fact that a few pounds of silver iodide released into the atmosphere in the form of fine particles can exercise a profound influence over the weather hundreds of miles away from the point of release. Clearly no private individual or group can be permitted to carry on operations over thousands or hundreds of thousands of square miles. The potentialities, both for good and bad, which attend silver-iodide seeding are so large that the development and use of this technique must be placed in the hands of the Federal Government. Despite Dr. Vonnegut's clear insight into the nature of the problem, the U.S. Congress never passed a statute regulating weather modification. (Havens, Jiusto, Vonnegut, 1978, p. 53)

earth. Over the last 25 years, the percentage of CO_2 in the

atmosphere has gone up by around 8 percent. Due to

having more CO_2 in the atmosphere, a greater amount of

heat is absorbed and kept, causing global temperatures to

rise. This greater amount of CO_2 has caused the

greenhouse effect, and could potentially continue to raise

temperatures beyond reasonable levels. As has been

shown, there are currently five ionosphere facilities, all

bouncing ELF Waves or other waves off the

ionosphere. With the in depth interest of the United States

Government in this technology, it makes other countries

rush to compete, such as Russia and the European

Community. And, there are articles throughout the

internet of small scientists and colleges putting up their

own ELF antennas to transmit these waves. If the United

States would just open up what we are doing through this

research, it may curb other smaller countries from

conducting Ionosphere Research, especially at an

uncontrolled level that may cause damage to the earth or it's Ionosphere.

Within the last year, the United States Government has pushed for increased openness of the Iranian Nuclear Facilities. [17] The United States and Israel has pushed the United Nations for openness of Syria's Nuclear Facilities. [18] Recently, the United States requested more transparency on a new Aircraft Carrier that China

---

[17] In May 2011, the world's global nuclear inspection agency, frustrated by Iran's refusal to answer questions, revealed that it possesses evidence that Tehran has conducted work on a highly sophisticated nuclear triggering technology that experts said could be used for only one purpose: setting off a nuclear weapon. Based on recent visits by inspectors, the agency also concluded that Iran's main production site at Natanz had recovered and was producing low-enriched uranium at rates slightly exceeding what it produced before being hit by the Stuxnet. Official American and Israeli estimates suggest Iran would not be able to produce a bomb until 2012, or more likely several years after that.   Article in the New York Times, August 28, 2011.

[18] Israeli intelligence agencies are aware of additional Syrian nuclear facilities, Defense Minister Ehud Barak said on Thursday, amid reports that Syria was harboring a uranium conversion reactor near the town of Marj as-Sultan, about 15 km. east of Damascus.
The German *Sueddeutsche Zeitung* newspaper on Thursday identified the location of the site, which is suspected of containing a small uranium conversion facility that is functionally related to the covert reactor at al-Kibar that the Israel Air Force destroyed in September 2007. The Jerusalem Post, "Israeli Intelligence Aware of Syrian Nuke Facilities," by Yaakov Katz, February 25, 2011.

introduced called the Varyag.[19] We specifically wanted to know why China suddenly has an interest in Aircraft Carriers. The United States expects North Korea, Somalia, Venezuela, and other countries to comply with United Nations inspections, and to be open on subjects that we may perceive as a threat.

It is because we expect transparency of perceived threats from other countries, that we should expect transparency of the HAARP facility. Furthermore, because weather patterns are rapidly changing throughout the world, we need to increase the transparency of this facility, and we need to demand inspections of other Ionosphere Research facilities.

---

[19] "We have had concerns for some time, and we've been quite open about them with regard to the lack of transparency from China regarding its power projection and its lack of access and denial of capabilities," State Department spokesperson Victoria Nuland told reporters on Wednesday. Article: US Wants More Transparency from China on New Aircraft Carrier, International Business Times, August 11, 2011.

In 2011, with twitter, internet, cell phones, and other instant media sources, there is an impossibility to keep just about every military movement, statement, new technology, and news story from being instantly transmitted; unless you are Iran, blocking internet access. Seemingly the last country to keep some secrecy is North Korea, and the US does a good job of knowing their movements even with limited communications. George Washington perhaps once said it best when he stated that "three men can keep a secret if two of them are dead." The best secrets today are often only half hidden, and the half that shows can create turmoil. In January, 2011 Russia stressed at a NATO Council meeting that transparency was paramount, and that it was important that any US-UN War Plans should not be directed at Russian interests.[20]

---

[20] The atmosphere at the latest session of the Russia-NATO Council was extremely tense. On several occasions, the Secretary-General had to suspend the discussion before the Council eventually worked out a compromise and approved two important amendments to its co-operation program. The first one stresses the need for the two parties to discuss the general direction of their military planning. This was our

Conclusion

The weather technology gained from the High

Frequency Active Auroral Research Program should be

openly published, to deter other countries and individuals

from performing sub-standard weather experiments,

possibly injuring the earth's eco-systems. Furthermore,

the data HAARP has obtained from its research into the

Ionosphere and ELF Waves should be openly published, so

other scientists are not redundant. With growing

technology in weather modification, it is becoming a moral

and ethical obligation to regulate weather experiments

---

initiative. Russia thinks that in order to really normalize Russia-NATO relations the two sides definitely should issue mutual assurances that their military plans will not be aimed against each other. This will help us avoid many unpleasant situations, such as the one we had recently when NATO plans to defend Poland and the Baltic States from Russia were made public. The second amendment says that we should finally move towards more serious and responsible co-operation in creating a theater missile defense system in Europe. "Russia and NATO should make their military plans transparent for each other," An Article in RT, January 27, 2011.

and document results.   Through Tesla's initial research,

we have created   a weapon greater than the atomic bomb

or a nuclear weapon. This weapon is possibly unmatched

in potential to destroy the world.   This weapon is called

weather modification, and the results could have

detrimental effects on an enemy when deployed correctly;

or deadly on us all if used by amateurs.

Science Projects

This writing was about HAARP, but it could have been

about many different types of scientific projects. The fact

is that there are superconductors being created to split

atoms, and other scientific projects that are being

conducted (some openly and some secretly) which have

lasting impacts on the society. These include genetic

engineering of plants, cloning of animals, especially sheep

(have humans been cloned?), and other weather

modification programs. Hitler was both a genius and a

lunatic when it came to science experiments. He used to cut open human beings when they were still alive for the sake of scientific experiments. It took a while for America to really understand how far he tilted the scale from genius to monster.

We spend so much time, energy, and technologies trying to change what is already made, to where we forget about what is important. We need peace in Israel and the Middle East. We need free, clean drinking water throughout the world. We need the true Jewish people to fall on their knees, and to beg God for forgiveness, and to fight to maintain what they have been given. And, we as American's need to prepare to support them in their time of need. Why could our smartest scientists and thinkers not be working on these tough challenges of tomorrow.

Our largest problem is patience. We want to know. We want to understand. We see this wonderful world and the moon and stars and we become fascinated with what is the make up of such. The truth is, God has and is all. He is the beginning and the end. He gave you and me the breath we breathe, and when it is time, he will have us quit breathing. We will all die and leave this earth. I have thrown a lot at you over the last 95(+) pages. What I would like to finish with is some thoughts on life itself:

These are just some things to think about:

- There may be a time when God chooses the Jewish people to lose as they have not lived up to the rules and obligations that he set before them. This happened frequently in the Old Testament.
- The pornography industry has done more for the destruction of America and the world in the last 40 years, than anything else, even drugs.
- Even David in the Bible, when he took it upon himself to conduct a census without God's permission, was punished by God.

- What punishment does a nation that condones homosexuality, abortion, divorce, adultery, corruption, and lying deserve?

- In John 3:16 it says "For God so loved the world, that he gave his only begotten son, that whosoever believeth in him, should not perish, but have everlasting life. For God sent not his son into the world to condemn the world, but that the world through him might be saved. He that believeth in him is not condemned: but he that believeth not is condemned already, because he hath not believed in the name of the only begotten Son of God."

- Psalms 23 says, "thou preparist a table for me in the presence of mine enemies.... "

- God gave us the land, the means to prosperity, the gold, the coal, the goodness of the sea. And, as we turn our back on him and think we can do it ourselves, he slowly destroys it, as he did Sodom and Gomorrah.

- As Napoleon Bonaparte once said, "the moral is to the physical, as 3:1."

- God uses both good and evil to accomplish his will.

- No matter what you ever read, know that God is in charge of both good and evil.

- The United States has a God given obligation as a strong nation to feed the hungry. We have a God given obligation to take care of the weak, and to protect the innocent. If you are American and you question this, then you are not a true American. For the true American's, from the beginning, were Christians. This faith from the beginning of our country is what is the driving force to our continued success. As the all-knowing eye is on the back of the dollar bill, along with the words,

"In God We Trust," so were the words in the founder's eyes. If you question me, which many will, get a copy of the Declaration of Independence and read it again for the first time. Our country has an internal compass of right and wrong. And, as the Bible says, he who is given much, much will be expected of him.

- God still knows who we are. He blesses us today as he blessed lands before us. And, he will make us suffer as payment for our sins as he made men before us. God gave us men who wrote the United States Constitution, which has constantly been under attack by liberals and hypocrites. However, no matter what you say about our government, there is nothing that beats it in the world. And, people die off the coast of Miami and on the borders of Mexico every day to get within the border of the United States.

- The United States, as a country, so far, has been blessed with little terrorism (except 9/11), a relatively low crime rate, a relatively low unemployment rate (although it is rising), and with opportunities for all. We have a minimum amount of dangerous storms, and a steady logistics system which provides fruits, vegetables, meats, tobacco, and other items to the market on a timely basis at a reasonable price. Who, as an individual, could sit down and design all of the systems that make up the free enterprise system in America and have them work as well as they do? The only one I know is the same being who created man in the first place, along with the heavens and the earth.

- America cannot work as a Socialist Country. We need Capitalism because it is what fuels economic growth and tax increase. Let's look at the money cycle of private enterprise versus public enterprise. The private enterprise person (small business owner, corporate worker, etc.) pays taxes from money they individually create by working with private capital. The public worker (government worker, corporation that is dependent on the government for business, etc.) pay taxes off government money (no new taxes are created). Small business creates more new wealth in America each year than anything else. Thus, the focus of government should be to ensure our small businesses succeed.

- The makeup of America was and is only through the inspiration and blessing of God. And, I am not saying that other countries are not blessed, because they are. However, it is my personal opinion that God has a special place in his heart for America, and blesses it based off how we react to his word and the world. However, here lately,

God has gotten to have become just a little sour

toward us as a nation. And, with good reason. We

openly flaunt homosexuality, which is stated

several times throughout the Bible that man shall

not be with man, nor for a woman to be with a

woman. He also says it is an abomination for a

woman to dress like a man. Here recently, high

level Officials have been supportive of getting rid

of "Don't Ask, don't tell in the military." Be

openly Gay in today's military?   When God

clearly speaks against homosexuality in the Bible?

I don't even know what an openly Gay person

would look like in the military, unless they wore a

special uniform that said, look at me, I'm Gay.

Why does their sin and downfall have to be

brought into my or my children's world?   I never

discuss with others in the military my sex life with

my wife. Why should Gays feel open to discuss

their sexual tendencies with me. When they give Gays rights to talk about their sex lives openly, they take away from my rights because I have to give up my religious beliefs to try to accept their way of life. Why is that fair? And, Gay sex in North Carolina is not even legal. It is considered sodomy. So, we have the Federal Government telling the State Government to break their own Laws.

- Our largest sin as American's is that we have to look, and by looking, we want to become. Victoria Secrets has built an empire of stores on that simple downfall of man. Muslim culture cover their women, to protect men from seeing enough of a woman to where there is lust in their heart.

- In Genesis, Chapter 11, God speaks of how the whole world was of one language and of one speech. And they made bricks and they said "go to let us build us a city and a tower whose top may reach unto heaven and let us make us a name. Lest we shall be scattered abroad amongst the surface of the whole earth." And the Lord said "behold the people is one, and they have all one language, and this they begin to do: and now nothing will be restrained from them which they have imagined to do." So the Lord scattered them abroad from them upon the face of all the earth, and they left off to build the city. Therefore the name of it is called Babel, because the Lord did there confound the language of all the earth and from there did the Lord scatter them abroad upon the face of the earth. We, today, through modern technology, media and lack of understanding, have put back together what God once deemed as threatening to him and his will. Very few people would listen to the words that we are threatening to God, but it may be true. You see, we were separated for a reason.

- We are destroying our own country , and possibly our world, because we are turning our back on what is Biblically right, and going toward what many believe is humanly a right because they don't look at the Bible and have understanding of God's word

- The Bible teaches us in Proverbs , Chapter 15, vs. 32 "He that refuseth instruction despiseth his own soul; but he that heareth reproof getteth understanding. The fear of the Lord is the instruction of wisdom; and before honor is humility."

- In Proverbs, Chapter 22, Vs. 4 it states, "by humility and the fear of the Lord are riches, and honor, and life."

- Have you ever been to a funeral, looked around, seen all of the family present, and asked yourself, "why don't we get together more often." At a funeral, usually a family will put aside petty differences and remember the deceased. Death brings us together. Right now, we as a nation are split between what is morally and ethically right, those who follow Christ, and those who are scientists, who believe that what man creates and deems right is right

- This nation was founded on Christianity. Our money says "In God We Trust." Our pledge of allegiance uses the words "one nation, under God." In fact, after the Civil War, it was almost voted in that this nation cannot survive except for the grace of Jesus be added to the Constitution.

- And, when a citizen chooses to hurt America, as in the Oklahoma bombings, God is the watchful eye. How did Timothy McVeigh get caught? Not through some in depth thought process of analysis of who did what, but through a local police officer doing his job, and thinking or being prodded, "that does not look right." This is how most crime is solved in America and in the world. God puts the right people in the right places at the right time, kind of like little birdies

- We give as a country, because we as a country and sound government understand that the only way to receive is through giving. America gives, and gives, and actually in many cases borrows to give. We understand that peace in our land is through peace and prosperity for all.

- It is often said that our government is leading the way toward us becoming a non-Christian nation. As a Police Officer, I will be the first to tell you that I have rarely ever seen a non-Christian Police

Officer. Oh, they are out there, including homosexuals and just non-believers. And, as a military officer in the Army reserves, I have rarely been to many staff meetings and plans meetings in Iraq or elsewhere to where the first words spoken were that of a Chaplains. In fact, as one questions the depth and gravity of Christ in our Nation, look at the front of most government buildings, and you will see an unfinished stone that is oddly out of place. The unsaid meaning of that stone is from both Psalms 118:22 and Matthew 21:42, as well as other places in the Bible, where Jesus states " the stone which the builders rejected, the same has become the head of the corner: this is the Lords doing, and it is marvelous in our eyes." Do you think it just chance this unfinished stone is at the head of school buildings and government buildings?   Or that perhaps at least a group of men and women have not forgotten our roots.

- The soundness and security of what America has, and is, is not from Gross National Product, from the strength of our armed forces, from the intelligence community and their work of gaining knowledge and understanding, or from a 40mm round in a Glock Pistol. The soundness and security of our great nation, the United States of America is from the group of older women and men who attend church every Sunday, who pray for the government, their families, and the needs of those around them, and who give money, food, shelter, and time to those in need and consistently become closer to Christ in their lives. You want to build a good country, help those in the church who are doing the Lords work. You want to build a great county: teach the children to be Christ like in words and deeds, and this next generation will not be worrying about how to stay ahead of the nuclear holocaust, but about what to wear to Church on Sunday, if they cleaned their room well enough, or about making better grades.

- The best way we as a nation can come together is to embrace our Christian heritage, to accept our evil past, to ask and received forgiveness, and to learn to do right. We need to teach our children moral values, our adults how to be parents, our leaders how to seek Christ, and all citizens on how to live right. Our political elections should be as much on who will seek advice from Christian leaders and God, than from their ability to speak. Our financial markets, banks, and lending institutions should place honesty, as the number one trait they require in new employees. And, they should immediately get rid of the unethical stock brokers, bond traders, government employees, and others who have problems with the truth. We in every way need to learn how to do the right thing. We need to learn to help our neighbor, and to give like we have never given. And we need to pray, that God will turn our hearts from evil, that we may not have to suffer grief. God put Jesus on this earth for one reason: the atonement of our sins. That those who believe in him as the Christ, will be forgiven of their sins. It is that simple. He was the sacrifice that took the place of all the animal sacrifices in the Old Testament. The scars remain, but there is new life after being saved.

- This freedom was actually forecasted by the Prophet Isaiah. Isaiah said in Chapter 1, verse 10-20: "Hear the word of the Lord ye rulers of Sodom; give ear unto the law of our God, ye people of Gomorrah. To what purpose is the multitude of your sacrifices unto me? Saith the Lord. I am full of the burnt offerings of rams and the fat of fed beasts, and I delight not in the blood of bullocks, or of lambs or of he goats. When you come to appear before me, who hath required this at your hand to tread my courts. Bring no more vain oblation; incense is an abomination to me. The new moons and Sabbaths, the calling of assemblies, I cannot away with. It is iniquity, even the solemn meeting. Your new moons and your appointed feasts, my soul hateth. They are a trouble unto me. I am weary to bear them. And, when you spread forth your hands I will hide mine eyes from you, yea when ye make many prayers, I will not hear, your hands are full of blood. Wash you, make you clean. Put away the evil of your doings from before my eyes, cease to do evil.

Learn to do well. Seek judgment, relieve the
oppressed, judge the fatherless, plead for the
widow. Come now and let us reason together,
saith the Lord. Though your sins be as scarlet,
they shall be as white as snow. Though they be
red like crimson, they shall be as wool. If ye be
willing and obedient, ye shall eat the good of the
land. But, if ye refuse and rebel, ye shall be
devoured with the sword, for the mouth of the
Lord hath spoken it."

- In Proverbs, Chapter 19, vs. 26, "He that
  wasteth his father, and chaseth away his mother, is
  a son that causeth shame, and bringeth reproach.
  Cease my son to hear the instruction that causeth
  to err from the words of knowledge."

- God is omnipresent. He sees and knows all.
  In Proverbs, Chapter 20, vs. 11 it is said, "even
  a child is known by his doings, whether his

work be pure, and whether it be right. The hearing ear and the seeing eye, the Lord hath made even both of them."

- We, both America and Israel, have the obligation to protect those around us who are weak, who may have been hurt by their government. We may be called upon to go to Somalia or Tunisia or many other places as a government to stop injustices that are occurring. We, as the United States of America, and Israel, Gods own people, are one and should know that what we do should be right. These other countries who run around and blow up their sons and daughters in the name of Allah, are wrong. I highly recommend if you never have done so, to take a walk on the battle ground of Yorktown, Virginia. This is where General George

Washington and General De Lafayette fought bravely to end the war of the American Revolution.

- As the Bible says, a man who is caught stealing that is hungry or thirsty, you can almost feel sorry for. But, he will wind up paying 4 times for that by which was taken. Jesus said, ask and it shall be given to you. God will not with hold that by which is good to you. And, you would be surprised at the generosity of people if you ask. Just ask. If someone turns you away and you are hungry, God will know that. Go to the next person and ask for food.

- We as a country may get back to the point to where there are some extremely poor families out there who need our help. If you have, you need to share. If you have not, you need to ask. When America was first being founded back in the late 1700's, there were many men who lost everything they had because they bet on land in the expansion of America West. During the Great Depression, there were masses of unemployed and desperate families. However, when everything else failed, we turned to God. America has a history of having poor people. America also has a history of having people who are willing to give.

- The United States Court System has set up a good system of protecting the innocent. First of all, it generally takes two or more witnesses to prosecute someone. Next, it generally takes evidence to tie someone to the crime. Next, there usually has to be a defined motive. And finally, there has to be an actual defined crime committed, before someone can be convicted.

- I don't think God ever wanted us to do without, or to need something and not to have it. From the very beginning, he gave Adam and Eve fruit to eat and no worries. Then when they sinned, he basically still gave them the tools and land to farm to grow food. He gave them cattle and meat. There was nothing we have ever lacked. When Moses took the Israelites out of Egypt into the desert for 40 years, God gave them water and manna. They had to ask, but it was given to them.

- Look at this great nation we have and the blessings that have been bestowed upon us. We have a fair set of laws and governance, we usually have a means to make a living, we usually have money in our pockets. If we lack, it is usually in the things we want, and not in the things we truly need.

- Also, in Islamic countries, they keep their women covered up. We in America think that this is because they are trying to hold them down, or that they are considered lower than men. In reality, it is because they understand that lust drives sin in a man's heart. If a man sees a woman and has lust for her, he has sinned, which could lead to more sin. If women are covered up, it at least reduces the chance of lust and coveting someone else's wife. We as American's could learn a thing or two from our Islamic brothers, or from Paul in the Bible. We, as American's and church going folk ourselves, have turned from that which we know is right and made it wrong for Hollywood's sake, as well as to appease to our need to see

- At the end of the Civil War, the Generals and other lawmakers from the North sat around and tried to think of what to do with former Southern President Jefferson Davis, while he was held prisoner at Fort Monroe, Virginia. While he was held prisoner, many women and men from the North found forgiveness in their hearts. He was soon set free and was never tried.

- Love the Lord your God with all your heart , and with all mind, and with all your soul.

- Do unto others as you would have them do unto you.

- According to Proverbs, Chapter 6, Verse 16, "these six things doth the Lord hate, yea, seven are an abomination unto him. A proud look, a lying tongue, and hands that shed innocent blood. A heart that deviseth wicked imaginations, feet that be swift in running to mischief, a false witness that speaketh lies, and he that soweth discord among brothers. "

- There are three things we should have to be close to God: (1) the fear of the Lord, and (2) wisdom, and (3) understanding.

- The fear of the Lord, according to Proverbs, Chapter 8, verse 13 states that "the fear of the Lord is to hate evil, pride, and arrogancy, and the evil way, and the forward mouth, do I hate."

- Wisdom comes from the Lord. In Proverbs, Chapter 2, Verse 6, the Bible says "For the Lord giveth wisdom, out of his mouth cometh knowledge and understanding. He layeth up sound wisdom for the righteous: he is a buckler to them that walk uprightly. He keepeth the paths of judgement, and preserveth the way of his saints. Then shall thou understand righteousness, and judgement, and equity; yea every good path. When wisdom entereth into thine heart, and knowledge is pleasant unto thy soul; discretion shall preserve thee, understanding shall keep thee. To deliver thee from the way of the evil man, from the man that speaketh forward things." Therefore,

to obtain wisdom, one should obtain knowledge of
the ways of God, by reading the Bible, and
practice right conduct, by living what you read.

- Understanding also comes from the Lord. One of
  the most significant parts of the Bible is when
  Solomon, who could have asked God for anything,
  asks for understanding. 1 Kings Chapter 8 says
  "And now, O Lord my God, thou hast made thy
  servant king instead of David my father; and I am
  but a little child: I know not how to go out or come
  in. And thy servant is in the midst of thy people
  (Israel) which thou hast chosen, a great people, that
  cannot be numbered nor counted for multitude.
  Give therefore thy servant an understanding heart to
  judge thy people, that I may discern between good
  and bad: for who is able to judge this thy so great a
  people? And the speech pleased the Lord, that

Solomon had asked this thing. And God said unto him, because thou hast asked this thing, and hast not asked for thyself long life, neither hast asked riches for thyself, nor hast asked the life of thine enemies: but hast asked for thyself understanding to discern judgment; behold I have given thee as wise and understanding heart, so that there was none like thee before thee, neither shall any arise like unto thee." Solomon went on to show that he was like none before him, or after him with the ability to discern good and evil.

- Jesus taught us how to pray in the Lord's Prayer, as he prayed "Our Father, who art in heaven, hallowed be thy name. Thy kingdom come, thy will be done, on earth as it is in heaven. Give us this day our daily bread, and forgive us our trespasses as we forgive those who trespass against us, and lead us not into temptation, but deliver us from evil, for thou are the kingdom, the power and the glory forever. Amen.

- The Old Testament gives us the foundation for a good Christian life. You see in it, the pre-cursors to Christ coming. Jesus was predicted by Isaiah, and several other prophets in the old testament.

- God usually does not start any action without a warning or a pre-cursor. The pre-cursor to Jesus was when God requested of Abraham to take his beloved son, Isaac, to the land of Moriah, and sacrifice him as a burnt offering to him for sin. The Bible never even says that Abraham questions this. He just gets up the next morning, saddles his ass, and takes his son to Moriah. On top of the mountain, his son says " behold the fire and the wood, but where is the lamb for the burnt offering," to which Abraham replies to him, "my son, God will provide himself a lamb for a burnt offering."

In Genesis Chapter 21, Verse 9 "And they came to the place which God had told him of, and Abraham built an altar there and laid the wood in order, and bound Isaac his son, and laid him on the altar upon the wood. And Abraham stretched forth his hand, and took the knife to slay his son. And the angel of the Lord called unto him out of heaven , and said, Abraham, Abraham: and he said , here am I. And he said, Lay not thine hand upon the lad neither do thou anything to him: for now I know that thou fearest God, seeing that thou hast not withheld thy son, thine only son from me. And Abraham lifted up his eyes, and looked, and behold behind him a ram caught in a thicket by his horns, and Abraham went and took the ram and offered him up for a burnt offering in the stead of his son. And Abraham called the name of that place, Jehovah-jireh, as it is called to this day. In the mount of the Lord it shall be seen." You see, God required in the early mosaic times a sacrifice to be slaughtered and killed and burnt on an altar as a sin offering. Early in Moses times, it was done by the individuals themselves. Later on, it became slaughtered and killed by the priest, as only the correct individuals were worthy to offer the sin offering.

- Jesus came and took all of this away. When Jesus was sacrificed on the cross, an individual, such as you and me, can accept him as our sacrifice, and our sins are forgiven us. Now, I read the Bible every year, and I understand from what it says how it works, but it is difficult to comprehend unless you just accept. Jesus came, lived a perfect life, and died on the cross for you and me. And, one day, he will return to earth and pick up those who are saved. Some people will believe this. Some people will not believe this. Even after he comes back, there will be those who will accept him and he will accept them into the kingdom of heaven. However, there will be those who will deny him to the end, just like the Jewish people did when he died on the cross.

- If you don't know Christ tonight, and I have not said anything that touched your heart, I can accept that. Honesty with this is the best answer. But, please get a Bible for yourself, and start on page 1 and read the entire book. What I have not convinced you of if you will open your heart to him, he will convince you of. You see, I have a lot of errors, faults, and am not perfect. God is perfect, and he wants you to live the way he had planned. Selah.

- A man who goes to war should have no trouble being a United States soldier as a Christian. The military that I am a part of is for the most part, made up of very honest and Christian men, who want to do the right thing. Like I said earlier, there are a lot of meetings that I have been to in the military that the first words that were spoken were a prayer to God that he would give us the knowledge, wisdom, and understanding to do that which needed to be done.

- God has sustained Muslims for thousands of years in the middle of the desert with little water or food. Many of these people want peace, and just want to be left alone. Al Qaeda lives in the middle of them not because the people want them there, but because they just want to be left alone. They figure, if we leave them alone, maybe they will leave us alone. It is a good argument, but one that sets us at war with each other for a long time. If Al Qaeda went away, then America would go away.

America only wants to do war with those who would attack our own or our allies.

- We as a country (US) have fought for our freedoms on the defensive up to this point. We have fired only if fired upon. However, after spending two years in Iraq, I have to question if we are doing the right thing. We are allowing a false understanding of a religion to attack us in the name of men. And, what really gets me is that the beginning of the Muslim religion started with them worshipping the same God we did. Allah was the God of Abraham. So, how did men with the beginning of praying to the same God, change the way they thought to where they see fit to blow up Americans. And do you remember, God blessed Abraham for being willing to sacrifice his son, so he spared his son and gave him a lamb. This lamb is the pre-cursor of Jesus. If only we could open your eyes.

- We invite thousands of Muslims in the United States each year to study at our Universities, allow them to build mosques in our country, allow them to have access to our health care, allow them to live in our country and buy land if they want. And how are we repaid; we are spit on. Muslims blow up our twin towers. They plot on how they will kidnap and kill our young soldiers, or visitors to their countries. They plan to attack Israel, the basis of our religion, and theirs if they looked deep enough. And they say they are doing it for the God of Israel? They have lost track of who Abraham was.

- At this point, I would have to say we (Americans) need to throw down our pitch forks and rakes and repel the invaders. If they choose to kill one of our children, then we should take every one of their students out of the United States and send them home. After all, they create these secret cells to plan terror at night, while they work and make money on our economy during the day. If they were truly blessed in the work they do, why would they hide while they did it. If they were doing God's work planning on killing the infidels, then they would be in his will. The truth is they are doing evil, and that is why they work in the dark. The truth is, they pray on young men and women with mental disorders, strap waist bombs on them, and then send them off to commit killings in a crowded Baghdad market. This is murder. This is not war. Thou shalt not kill.

- This goes for drug dealers in Mexico also. I have never been as upset as when the Mexican drug cartel killed a Christian Husband and wife, doing the Lord's work in Mexico, just so they could steal a truck from them. Why did they need to kill the man and woman for a truck? If they bomb our cities, we will destroy them completely. We will completely and utterly destroy the remembrance of them from the face of the earth. You say, that is not the Christian thing to do. We have been doing the Christian thing with them for 1000 + years. They don't get it. They don't get that we are trying to live peacefully with them. They don't get that we are trying to help them build better lives for themselves and their families. They don't get that we have given money, time, and countless lives so that they can worship and live with freedoms. And what do they do? They allow drug dealers to live in their yards.

- And, to top that off, we went against every principle of warfare since the beginning of time. When troops go to war, they are to live off the country they invade. We should have taken all the oil and all the assets from Iraq and stripped it dry to pay for coming over there. Instead, what did we do, we gave . We gave and gave and gave, and now that we have hurt ourselves through giving to the Iraqis, we continue giving. And, you would think that the Iraqi government would want to repay us by giving us discount oil or other resources. Instead, they take their oil and sell it to Russia or others.

- As you worship today, I would ask that you pray on your own that God will give you a plan for your life. I would ask that you would pray for our Islamic brothers that they would receive knowledge and understanding. However, I would ask that you as a fellow brother in Christ become fully armed in the knowledge that you may be called upon one day to fight for that by which is right in America. For freedom of worship. For the right to bear arms. For the right to live freely in one of the greatest nations that has ever lived. It was never the government that made America strong, although we have been blessed with a strong central government. It was the individual, who made a living through his own life without ever needing government assistance. It was the embodiment of everything that Harley Davidson, an American owned motorcycle company, existed for.

- "Ask not what your country can do for you. Ask what you can do for your country." I believe these words to be from a speech given by President John Kennedy. It is time we as Christians see again the light. We will not be able to change everyone, but we must come together and change ourselves, and through our words and deeds, perhaps we can change others. There are men that will always be slothful with work; these men I just don't know.

Thomas Jefferson once said something to the effect that the fastest way to destroy a country is to make those willing to work pay for those who are not. But, for those of us who can, the time to rebuild is now. We have to accept there always have been and always will be people who are unable and unwilling to work. Get it in your mind you cannot change that. What you can change is yourself and those around you. If you work for the government, Receive disability or any other subsidies, talk to your Senators and Congressmen about cutting your pay to 78% of its current value so we can once again balance our deficit. And, if you can, start a small business and hire someone else. We can fix this mess we are in financially if you and I will help.

- We have some very honest and talented people in America. We have people who invent, who write, who study and find understanding in Science, who create. All of these hard working and honest people are being slighted by the people who will steal, market, and profit off their work. It is like you have two kids in school. One studies all night to pass a math test. The other cheats off the paper of the student who studied all night. Are we, America, ready to accept the cheater as worthy of the same grade as the one who studied all night. Unfortunately, some of America will say, yes.

- It is God who gave us a mind, a body, a spirit, direction, air to breathe, and freedom. And, he can as easily give it away. If you read in the Old Testament, God put the Israelites in bondage (slavery) in Egypt. Then, God called Moses, who did not want to lead, to get them out. He put them in slavery because they were wicked. If the Israelites would have chosen a leader to get them out of slavery, it would not have been probably Moses, as he was not the best speaker or politically connected. In fact, Moses questioned God when God told him to represent the people. He did not feel worthy or noteworthy enough to lead the Israelites. He finally talked God into giving him an assistant, Aaron. Moses, who was led by God, inspired by God, and given by God for this purpose, eventually won the freedom of the Israelites and took them into the desert. From the beginning of their freedom, they started to complain. (Some people don't deserve freedom). They did not have water, or they did not have food or they did not have this or that. Freedom is not free. The Israelites could have stayed and ate well in bondage with the Egyptians. But, their destiny was to follow Moses and become free. However, God did not lead them through easy land, such as the Philistines, because "Lest the people repent when they see war and return to Egypt." Exodus 13:17. We need to teach our children to follow God, even when times are tough. He will see you through, in his time frame and according to his will.

- We are also getting ready to go through one of the toughest times socially that we have ever seen. We will see a split not only between blacks and whites, as well as other races, but also between workers and non-workers. We will see tension arise as the Democrats continue pushing for subsidized health care, housing, education, and income off the backs of workers who are already working 2-3 jobs to make ends meet. I am white and know of few truly prejudice white people against blacks: but I know a lot of both blacks and whites that are truly prejudice against the welfare system that they work to subsidize. Men and women who work sometimes 2 and 3 jobs to support their families are tired of paying more so others can sit there and do nothing. Children today should be taught the importance of working, and giving without expecting anything in return.

- We are getting ready to see our economic debt, to pay for these subsidies, place America in the worst financial shape that we have ever been in. The Bretton-Wood Act, which backed the dollar with gold for many years, will have to be re-enacted to back the US Currency because no one trusts it. We, America, the land of the free and the home of the brave, are about to become a 3rd world country if we don't change. We need to back our scientists and protect their rights to their inventions. We need to take charge of our publically held companies and make them responsible economically and socially. And, we need to tear our clothes, wail, and beg God for forgiveness for the sins that we have done. For we took that by which God gave us and that was good, and corrupted it to the point that we are all confused. We took that which was wrong, and made it right. We took that by which is right, and made it wrong. And until we gain God's forgiveness, he will not heal our land or bless our work. And, this next generation, unless things change, may not even know who God is. We need an awakening in America today. We need families to understand that our futures depend on them being moral and learning as much as possible in school, so they can survive being an honest generation. If we do nothing with our economy, at one day in the future,

we will be so broke to where our country cannot
pay any benefits. We have gotten to do the right
thing.

- I truly don't even know how one could become
homosexual. Why some man would want to stick
his penis up some other guys butt; it does not even
make logical sense. Or one woman kiss another
woman. Besides the grossness of it, God said
several times through the Bible that man was not to
be with man, but that a man should leave his home,
and join with woman, and that the two shall be as
one. Also, that women should not work that
which is unnatural among themselves. But, since
Old Testament times and before, men and women
have done this. Just like Al Qaeda, homosexuals
want to be smarter than God. It is my opinion as
well as many Physicians and Psychiatrists (who

have backbones to state such) that Homosexuality is a Psychological Disorder.   The argument for this is " well I am just attracted to my own sex." Because you feel weird does that make it right. "Well I just felt like killing twelve women." Because you feel like it does that make it right. Well, I just like dating little girls. Does that make it right? Well, I just felt like blowing up a building and murdering innocent people.   Just because you feel like doing something does not change what God sees as right and wrong.

- If you look outside every morning, the sun rises, and in the afternoon, the sun goes down. The moon appears in the evening skies at the level of what it is through the month (i.e. crescent, full, etc.). The seasons change, and every year we have a Spring. The stars align in their constellations, and animals and fish go North and South every year with the

seasons. There is a balance of nature.
Homosexuality throws the human race off balance.
God created for almost every man, a female of
generally the same age and race as him as a spouse.
It is natural.

- You see these married gay people on television.
They think they are smarter than what God has
created, the natural family. They have gone and
married someone of their own sex, and then
adopted kids and say they are a "family." Some of
them go and get artificially inseminated with a
turkey baster shooting sperm in their vagina. Why,
do we, think something stupid like that outsmarts
God's original plan, which is as natural as the sun
rising? Why could you not see what is natural and
not. God created us all. Why would any human
being think he or she could outsmart his design.

This goes for weather systems also.

- I think God was as clear as possible in Sodom and Gomorrah. God sent an angel to see what was happening in the town. Two angels arrive, and visit Lot. Men see them enter, believe them to be men, and want to have sex with them. Lot offers them his daughters, because he wants to protect the angels. They refuse, and only want the men (who are really angels in disguise). Lot winds up giving them his concubine. They wind up raping and beating her, and leaving her to die. The next morning, the Angels tell Lot to get his family, leave Sodom and Gomorrah and don't look back. Sarah looks back and she becomes a pillar of salt. Sodom and Gomorrah is no more. Recently in Oakland, California about 6 males raped a 15 year old female for about 30 minutes while others watched. After They were finished, it took almost another 30 minutes before anyone called 911 for help for the female, who just lied on the ground.

- Do you remember the story of the prodigal son. He wanted his inheritance before his father died. His father gave it to him and he went and spent it all. He wound up having to feed swine to survive. When he finally came to his senses, he went back home and his father welcomed him and cut the fatted cow. That is how God is. You may have left the protection of his home because of sin, but he stands ready to take you back. You just have to ask, and to turn from your evil ways, and sin no more. You will still have lusts, desires, wants, feelings of guilt; you cannot handle them but when you give your life over to God, and ask for your forgiveness of sins through the blood of Jesus, it is done.

- America, wake up from this long dream that you are under. Everything is not alright. We are under attack by evil because we have invited it in. We need the country to turn from its past sins, and to ask for forgiveness. For the enemy we fight, is designed to destroy us. We need God in this battle, as we have always needed him. Please, if not for yourself, for others; turn your ways back to that which is right; ask God for forgiveness, and live a correct life. For only through us asking for forgiveness and turning from our evil ways will our land be healed and our children live in peace.

- One of the largest downfalls of man is his pride. He looks at what he has built and gives no credit to

God, and therefore God takes it away from him. There are several passages throughout the Bible to where God talks about how he hates pride, and destroys men for it. But, most likely you can look into your own life and think of times when you have acted proud of something you have accomplished, gotten, or purchased and it was taken away from you quickly. Pride is the downfall of man and countries. When an individual or a country believes they are something, that is when they are destroyed. Being humble is the key to this. In fact, this is one of the keys to life, to act humbly and to serve.

Conclusion

Many people have a natural inclination to disagree that God is the ultimate and only creator of all things. They use such arguments as dinosaurs, Cro-Magnums and Neanderthal Man, and time passages. They see on television Christian's being portrayed as weak and as stupid. Hollywood does a great job of destroying the image of the Christian American.

However, what atheists fail to ever come up with is where the very first DNA came from to create these humans. They tried the infamous Big Bang Theory. But, where did the rocks or whatever else that collided come from. The fact is, there is no argument that can beat a creator, God. And, the Bible starts with that in mind.

Genesis 1:1 states "in the beginning God created the heaven and the earth."

The Bible in Genesis speaks of giants in the land. In the book of Genesis, it states "And it came to pass, when men began to multiply on the face of the earth, and daughters were born unto them, that the sons of God (angels) saw the daughters of men that they were fair; and they took them wives of all which they chose. . . .There were giants in the earth in those days; and also after that, when the sons of God came in unto the daughters of men (had sexual relations with them), that they bare children to them, the same became mighty men which were of old, men of renown" (Gen.6:1-4). The additional issue that man has with the skulls that have been found in Peru and elsewhere and their contradiction with the timeline used in the Bible, one only has to understand that. Also, in Act 1:7 he said to them, It is not for you to know the times or the seasons, which the Father has put in His own authority."

If you have any doubts about God, his imperial goodness, his desire to give you a good and pleasurable and honorable life in his time, then argue with me after you have read the entire Bible. Read from Page (1) through the end, at a pace to where you can understand (5 or so pages a day), and then come back and argue with me. I believe through this reading assignment, you will find out who God truly is, and why his son is so important to our country, our economy, and our future.

May God bless you, your family, and the United States of America

REFERENCES

(1) Arfken, G. Mathematical Methods for Physicists, (Third Edition), Academic Press, New York, 1985.

(2) Air Force Geophysics Laboratory and Navy Office of Naval Research, Joint Services Plans and Activities, HAARP: HF Active Auroral Research Program, February 1990.

(3) Aquino, Fran De, High Power ELF Radiation Generated by Modulated HF heating of the Ionosphere Can cause Earthquakes, Cyclones, and Localized Heating, Maranhao State University, Physics Department, S.Luis/MA, Brazil, Copyright 2011.

(4) Battis, James; Pedersen, Todd; Bernhardt, Paul; Selcher, Craig; Ohab, John; "Armed with Science: Research and Applications for the Modern Military," Episode Number 56,

Department of Defense Webcast Subject: The High Frequency Active Research Program (HAARP), a Joint Project of the Air Force and Naval Research Laboratories," 24 February 2010.

(5) Beal, J.B. (1996). "Bio systems liquid crystals and potential effects of natural and artificial electromagnetic fields (EMFs). Second Annual Advanced Water Sciences Symposium, Exploratory Session 1, Dallas, TX.

(6) Belyaev, P.P., S.V. Polyakov, V.O. Rapoport, and V.Yu. Trakhtengerts, The ionosphere Alfvén resonator, J. Atmos. Terr. Phys., 52 (9), 781-788, 1990.

(7) Bering, (Lysak, 1991)E.A., and J.R. Benbrook, Intense 2.3 Hz electric field pulsations in the stratosphere at high auroral latitude, J. Geophysical. Res., 100(A5), 7791-7806, 1995.

(8) Bertell, Rosalie, "Background on the HAARP Project," Global Policy Forum,

November 5, 1996.
http://www.globalpolicy.org/socecon/envron
ment/weapons/htm}

(9) Bliokh, P.V., Nikolaenko, A.P., Filippov, Yu. F., Schumann Resonances in the Earth-Ionosphere Cavity (London, 1980).

(10) Britt, Robert Roy (2003). "Sun's Output Increasing in Possible Trend Fueling Global Warming."

(11)Chossudovsky, Michel (2004), "The Ultimate Weapon of Mass Destruction: Owning the Weather for Military Use," www.globalresearch.com , 27 September 2004.

(12) Chossudovsky, Michel (2000). "Washington's New World Order Weapons Have the Ability to Trigger Climate Change." 11-26-2000. The Globalization of Poverty, Common Courage Press.

(13) Farina, Almo (2011). "An Essay on the Relationship of Warfare Ecology to General Ecology," NATO Science for Peace and Security Series C: Environmental Security.

(14) Fitrakis, Bob (2002). "Scary HAARP Music: Add Russia's Duma to the list of those worried about U.S. weather experiments, August 22, 02, Columbus Alive. http://www.columbusalive.com/2002/200208 22/082202/08220205.html

(15) Florini, Ann, "A New Role for Transparency," Contemporary Security Policy, vol. 18, no. 2 (August 1997), p. 51.

(16) Framework Convention on Climate Change (UNFCCC), 1992 Earth Summit in Rio de Janeiro
(17) Gates, Robert M., Quadrennial Defense Review Report, February 2010.

(18) "HAARP Research and Applications," Washington, D.C. Technical Information Division, Naval Research Laboratory, 1990.

(19) Havens, B.S., Juisto, J.E. , Vonnegut, B; Early History of Cloud Seeding, New Mexico Institute of Mining and Technology, State University of New York at Albany and G.E.C.

(20) Hays, Peter L.; Transparency, Stability, and Deception: Military Implications of Commercial High Resolution Imaging Satellites in Theory and Practice, International Studies Association Annual Convention, Chicago, 21-24 Feb 2001.

(21) Kasper, Beth, The End of Secrecy? Military Competitiveness in the Age of Transparency, Occasional paper number 23, Center for Strategy and Technology, Air War College, Air University, August 2001.

(22) Long, Matthew; Lorenz, Allen; Rodgers, Greg; Tapio, Eric; Tran, Glenn; Jackson, Keoki; Twiggs, Robert, A Cubesat Derived Design for a Unique Academic Research Mission in Earthquake Signature Detection, Stanford University, Aeronautics and Astronautics.

(23) Lysak, R.L., Feedback Instability of the Ionosphere resonant cavity, J. Geophysics Res., 96(A2), 1553-1568, 1991.

(24) Lysak, R.L., Generalized model of the Ionosphere Alfvén resonator, Auroral Plasma Dynamics I, in Geophysics Monograph Ser.,

vol. 80 (R.L. Lysak, ed.), pp. 121-128, American Geophysical Union, Washington, D.D., 1993.

(25) Mackie, Randall L. (Personal Author), GSY-USA Inc. San Francisco, California (Corporate Author), Imaging of Underground Structure Using HAARP, http://handle.dtic.mil/100.2/ADA398268 DTIC: Information for the Defense Community, February, 1999 48 pages.

(26) National Earth Science Teachers Association, via website, http://www.windows2universe.org/earth/Atmosphere/ion_solar_effect.html

(27) Obama, Barack, National Security Strategy, May 2010.

(28) Polk, Charles, "Schumann Resonances," CRC Handbook of Atmospherics , I, 111-177

(29) Polyakov, S.V., and V.O. Rapoport, Ionosphere Alfvén resonator, Geomagnetism and Aeronomy., 21, 1981.

(30) Rembert, Tracey, Discordant HAARP: The Air Force Is Preparing to Militarize the Ionosphere with Electrifying Results, The Environmental Magazine, 23 pages, 1997.

(31) Robinson, Jana, Transparency and Confidence-Building Measures for Space Security, Space Policy, Volume 27, Issue 1, February 2011, Pages 27-37.

(32) Rowland, H.L. , Simulations of ELF Radiation Generated By Heating the High Latitude D-Region, Naval Research Laboratory, Washington, D. C.
(33) Sátori, G., Szendröi, J., and Vero, J., "Monitoring Schumann Resonances--I. Methodology," Journal of Atmospheric and Terrestrial Physics, 58 (13), 1996: 1475-1481.

(34) Schrage, Michael, Perfect Information and Perverse Incentives: Costs and Consequences of Transformation and Transparency, Security Studies Program Working Paper, Massachusetts Institute of Technology, E38-600, May 2003.

(35) Sentman, D.D., Approximate Schumann resonance parameters for a two-scale-height

ionosphere, J. Atmos. Terr. Phys.,52, 35, 1990.

(36) Sentman, D.D., Schumann resonance spectra in a two-scale-height earth-ionosphere cavity, J. Geophysical. Res., 101, 9479, 1996.

(37) Sentmen, D.D., "Schumann Resonances" in Handbook of Atmospheric Electrodynamics, (ed. Volland), Vol. I, 267-295. Boca Raton: CRC Press, 1995.

(38) Sprenger, Sebastian, GIG CONOPS Stresses Interoperability with Non-DOD Agencies, Allies, Inside the Pentagon, September 39, 2005.

(39) Shactman, Noah, Sky Lab, Wired Magazine, 8 pages, August 2009.

(40) Standler, Rondal B. , History and Problems in Weather Modification, 2002, as found on web page http://sguforums.com/index.php?topic=4018.90.

(41) Stephens, Brett, What Ahmadinejad Knows, The Wall Street Journal, 28 September 2010

(42) Werlhof, Claudia Call for a "Planetary Movement for Mother Earth," International Goddess-Conference, "Politics and Spirituality," Castle Hambach, Germany 29 May 2010.